NON-STOP

CULTIVATING AN UNSTOPPABLE FAITH IN THE MIDST OF ADVERSITY

NATHAN ROUSE

DEDICATION

This book is dedicated to my wife, Erin; whose constant love and support has helped me overcome fear, discouragement and failure in my own life. I love you with all my heart.

ACKNOWLEDGMENTS

M any contributed to making this book a reality. I want to sincerely thank the following for generously investing in this project: my friend and uncle, Danny Holley, Joe and Lara Nutt, Paul and Sharon Berry, Pastor Kris and Cheryl Weiss, Wayne Martin with BluFishWorx, Terry Allen, Ann and Leo Kahlich, Patricia Williamson, Craig and Starr West, Tracey Maxwell, Jeff Holley, Carl Holley, Janine Garner, Chris and Lisa Avery, Scott and Darlene Zeitler, Johnny and Jennifer Wyatt, Tammy Darling, Pastor Lenny and Mariam Corliss, Tim and Suzanne Hughes, Gail Rose, Matthew and Becky Miller. Special thanks to my editor, Court Dudek and my cover designer, J. P. Tanner.

CONTENTS

CONTENTS

INTRODUCTION

Quitting is not an option!

This sounds good in the movies, but it's just not true. Of course it's an option. It's an option you and I face every day. People quit all kinds of things for all kinds of reasons: mental and physical exhaustion, discouragement, disillusionment . . . the list goes on.

Most of you have known what it's like to feel like you're at the end of your rope with nothing left in the tank. Maybe you're there now. Maybe you're only putting one foot in front of the other because someone else is counting on you or you just plain don't want to be humiliated by giving up the fight.

I've been there. A couple of years ago after a rough day of ministry, I wanted to hit a major interstate and just drive until I ran out of gas. I believe my exact words were, "I am done." Thankfully, I didn't act on that impulse. This passage of scripture came to my rescue:

"He gives power to the faint, and to him who has no might he increases strength. Even youths shall faint and be weary, and young men shall fall exhausted; but they who wait for the Lord shall renew their strength; they shall mount up with wings like eagles; they shall run and not be weary; they shall walk and not faint" (Isaiah 40:29–31).

"Even youths grow tired and weary . . ." Even the most energetic in life get weary. You are not less than a Christian because your physical, emotional and spiritual tank is running low. Christians need to begin to see this as a normal part of life. Our resources are naturally depleted by living life.

Over the last twenty years in pastoral ministry, I have met countless people who were stuck on the side of the road who felt "done" with life. This book is for all those that have been held back by fear, discouragement and failure. This book is for all those who want to be able to break through these real life obstacles in the future and cultivate an unstoppable faith in the midst of it all. If you've wanted to not be sidelined by life's difficulties, this book is for you!

I've found that when I stop and sit down with those who have stopped on the side of the road in their spiritual faith, many times they're asking the same question, "God, where are you? I needed you, and you didn't show. I cried out to you in my darkest moment, and got nothing."

I've said those very words myself. Actually, I yelled them. (More about that later). The point is I'm not writing this book from theory. I'm writing after countless valleys and heartbreaks. I know what it is to be on the ropes taking body blow after body blow hoping that the God in your corner will throw in the towel to make the proverbial beating stop. Some of these knockout punches were brought by individuals, some by just life being life, but honestly most were unfortunately of my own doing. That's hard to admit, even now.

However, God has given me an unimaginable gift. A gift that I know many of you are in desperate need of. Hope. Hope that there can be something meaningful after you've picked up all the pieces. My prayer is you'll experience God's love and grace bursting over the horizon like a cloudless, blue sky, sunrise in your life.

If you're reading and right now finds you in a good season without any obstacles to hurdle, first let me say, ENJOY IT! Seriously, savor the calm waters. But, let me challenge you to allow this book to put some tools in your life toolbox for when the rapids of life hit. I want to invest in those moments that I know are on their way.

Let me challenge you to not put this off. Go ahead and jump in. I don't want you to spend one unneeded moment paralyzed by fear, discouragement, and failure in this short life. God has a rock solid peace on the other side of all of this. Trust me.

Oh . . . before you turn the page. Can we make a promise to one other?

Can we commit to being honest? I'll let you look behind the curtains of my life: the good, the bad, and the ugly in the hope that you'll allow yourself to be honest with where you and God truly are in life.

You with me?

Good. Let's get started.

CHAPTER 1

KILLER OF DREAMS AND CALLINGS

*Success is not final, failure is not fatal: it is
the courage to continue that counts.*

—Winston S. Churchill

My breakthrough happened while eating a quarter-pounder at McDonald's. No doubt it was an awkward place for a life altering moment. My oldest son sat nibbling on some chicken nuggets dug out of a happy meal and my youngest son was seeing how much distance he could get throwing French fries. Usually, I would have been scrambling to gather the aforementioned fries, but I was taken aback with how quickly my eyes were welling up with tears. I looked across the table at my wife who had unknowingly just placed a key of life into the proverbial padlock that held my chains of bondage.

She had simply said, "Don't you think it's time you go back to doing what you were called to do?"

My mind scrambled for an answer. I didn't have one. Words failed me. I looked down at my burger for counsel . . . nothing.

My wife continued to press, "I think it's time for us to move forward."

I know what you're thinking. What's the big deal with "Let's move forward?", but for you to better understand this moment I need to take you back sixteen years.

I came busting out of Bible College with the energy of a thoroughbred. I burned with white hot zeal and a consuming desire to change the world. What that looked like, I had no idea, but I knew the world needed changing. I had been blessed by God with tons of raw talent. I could sing pretty well, and I was comfortable talking to people whether it was one-on-one or a large crowd. On a deep heart level, I loved people no matter where they were in life. It seemed I was wired for compassion. I was made to be a pastor.

Unfortunately, I had spent much of my Bible College years focused on dating, friends, having a good time, and my studies (in that order). I didn't realize that as I left school with my beloved undergrad degree, I was sorely lacking in a much needed life skill: the ability to take a life punch. I was naïve to my own malformation. I thought talent and desire was enough. I was about to find out it wasn't.

I met *the* woman my now best friend and wife in August of 1996. At the time we both didn't think much of it, but a year later I was fully aware of her and my pursuit was at full tilt. My efforts were rewarded as we were engaged to be married in March of 1998. To sum it up, Erin is a beautiful, thoughtful, and practical woman. It was this powerful combination that drew me to her then and still does today.

However, just before the happiest day of our lives came the saddest. Erin's father, Ronnie, passed away from a stroke two weeks before we were to walk down the aisle. I had taken an associate pastor position in Kansas when I got the news. It was devastating. In a time when there should have been great anticipation with showers and gifts, now there was only grieving and the difficult decision of whether to move forward with or put off the wedding. Erin's mother, Donna, encouraged us to move forward. By God's grace we muddled through and still enjoyed smiles and laughter on our wedding day.

I was late to my wedding. My wife had given me a specific time to show up for the ceremony and I blew past that time by over an hour. As I rushed to get ready, I cut myself shaving. What I thought was a small nick, looked like I had hit my carotid artery. I could not stop the bleeding. With the look my bride to be gave me when I pulled up late, I was beginning to wonder if I should just let myself bleed out.

With half a toilet paper roll on my face I made my way over to the church auditorium for pictures. The photographer thought my tissue plied face was funny so he had all the groomsmen do the same to their faces for their group shot with the bridesmaids.

Pretty soon the wedding got started, and I found myself standing on the platform in front of a sea of people. My knees were literally shaking. My palms felt like water hoses had been hooked up to them by way of Niagara Falls. Half-way through the ceremony my nerves were lifted by a well-planned practical joke by my groomsman. They secretly stole my dress shoes and wrote "HELP ME" on the soles so that the audience would be telegraphed the mayday when we knelt for prayer. It was priceless.

Yet, as my wife and I began to make our vows, a life altering truth hit me: "I have no idea what I'm doing." That wouldn't be the last time I used those words in reference to being a husband.

I'm convinced my wife drew the short end of the straw. She thought she was marrying a strong, confident guy that had life and his calling all figured out. What she and I both didn't know was that I was backing up a U-Haul truck of insecurity and unhealed wounds to our marriage.

As we moved boxes in to our first apartment in Garden City, KS, we were also stepping in to our first pastorate with great anticipation. While these were still difficult days following Erin's Dad passing, we looked forward to making a life together. My first few weeks on the job as a pastor revealed to me that I honestly had no idea what I was doing. I compensated for this by turning up my outward confidence, walking quickly down hallways as if I had something important to get to, and calling people who actually knew what they were doing. My first six months I faked it till I made it.

Things began to take off in our youth and college ministry. A youth group of seven students soon became forty. Students were coming to faith in Christ, being baptized in water and the Spirit. Our college ministry on a small college campus across the street from the church was taking off and students' lives were being changed. Everything seemed to be going just as I had planned. Well, almost everything.

Erin and I didn't know that the church we were serving in that first year was hurting internally. So I was surprised when my good friend and senior pastor at the time, Kent Anderson, slipped out of his office during a board meeting looking like he had seen a ghost saying, "You're up. We'll talk after." Kent's demeanor didn't boost my confidence as I walked into my first annual review of the board. The board had instituted this practice after feeling like they needed to "buckle down" on their pastors. A previous pastor had taken advantage of his position by misusing church funds for personal and inappropriate expenses. The board's reaction while understandable, ended up swinging to the extreme as they turned to mistrust and micromanagement as their compass.

As I sat in my normal chair across from the board, I noticed that not one of them would make eye contact with me, except for one, (for anonymity's sake I'll call him Derk) and his face wasn't welcoming. I wasn't surprised it was Derk leading the charge. Soon I was handed my "review". The board had acquired a copy of an evaluation form for teachers and were using this as their review instrument. Right away I could tell this wasn't going to be helpful. Most of the categories evaluated on the sheet had nothing to do with what I did as a pastor: Uses Assigned Curriculum, Is Prompt to Bus and Cafeteria Duties, Submits Student Grades Promptly, etc. To top it off, the highest score you could receive in any category was "satisfactory". It was definitely not designed to inspire.

As I fumbled through the unsigned reviews, printed at the bottom of each page was a list of where I was "failing". Here were their main complaints:

- Office Desk is messy regularly
- Comes in late every Thursday morning

- Is not helpful when duty calls for him to step up and help

I looked up stunned and was about to speak, when (surprise) Derk beat me to it, "Nathan, do you want to speak to those main points at the bottom of the page?"

"I can try." I said nervously.

I explained that I indeed knew I had a messy desk. Guilty as charged! (I was a twenty-three year old Youth Pastor. In most states in the U.S. a messy desk is part of the job description. I didn't share this because they didn't seem to be in the mood). I told them I'd work on making sure it looked more organized. As for coming in late on Thursdays, I explained that Pastor Kent (my boss) had given me permission to do so because of my Wednesday night ministry schedule.

Derk interjected, "Nathan, we all come to church on Wednesday nights, but we don't go in to work late the next day because of it!"

Frustrated, I shot back, "Long after you all leave and I shut everything down and lock up the church, Erin and I then drive over to the college campus to lead our Chi Alpha service that starts at nine p.m. We usually don't get home until 11:00 or 11:30."

Kent jumped in, "So, yes, I told Nathan he could come in at ten a.m. on Thursdays."

"We didn't know that," said Todd, one of the friendliest board members.

"You didn't ask," said Kent, perturbed.

"As for the 'not stepping up when duty calls for it', I don't know what you mean. I'm the first one here and the

6

last one to leave," I said, getting back to the final written grievance.

Again, Derk spoke up, "You don't know what we mean? How about the time the gym flooded and you and Kent came down and popped your head in the door and saw me sucking up two inches of water off the entire gym floor with my industrial vac! (Derk had a carpet cleaning business).

"What did you want him to do? Get out there with a mop? It was almost ankle deep!" Kent fired back.

I further explained, "Derk, the reason I left wasn't because I wasn't willing to help. We found out about the flooding of the gym right before I had to meet with some school administration officials. I was asking them to give one of our students another chance after he'd been expelled."

"We didn't know that either," said Todd as he looked over at Derk ashamedly.

"Again, you didn't ask," said Kent exasperated.

Derk, feeling the tide turning, went for the jugular. "Regardless, can you tell us what you actually do here? What do we pay you for? Where are the changed lives?"

"What do you mean?" I asked.

"We brought you here to change the lives of our teenagers. We're just not seeing it. I'm just gonna say it, I think you're here for the money," said Derk with a grimace.

That hurt.

Let me just pause my story here for a moment to give you some insight. While there are some ministers out there "just doing it for the paycheck" (we've all heard the stories), most pastors truly love the Lord and their people. It's certainly not the paycheck that's out of this world. I would say the most comical and hurtful thing you could say to a pastor is you're in it for the money. My recommendation, don't say it.

Back to my story.

With tears welling up in my eyes, I said, "I guess I don't know what you mean by changed lives. Students are coming to Christ and being baptized, and they're walking away from destructive behaviors. We're reaching part of the town that the church has never reached before. We've gone from a handful of students to a room full. What else can I do?"

The room fell silent for about ten seconds.

"Would it help if I recorded my hours and activities in detail and gave you a weekly report?" I said.

"That'd be great," said Todd.

When the meeting was over, I hurriedly left the church. I just wanted to get out of there. I pulled into my driveway and walked into the apartment to find Erin sitting on the couch watching a show. She could clearly see I was upset and turned the TV off. I came over, slumped down by her, and began to recount to her the events of the evening.

"They said I was doing this for the money," I told her as I began to tear up.

I was heartbroken. In just two hours my entire naïve view of ministry had been wrecked. Apparently not everyone was part of the "Nathan Fan Club." It was my first real taste of discouragement in ministry. As you can imagine I didn't sleep well that night. A small seed of thought crept in seeking germination, "What if I'm not really called into full-time ministry?"

I dragged myself out of bed the next morning not wanting to be "late" just in case a board member drove by. I remember thinking to myself, *this is not what I signed up for.* After some brief reflection in my office, I decided I would create a binder for each board member and catalogue every minute of my day. I mean *every* minute: prayer time, sermon prep, music and worship prep, counseling appointments, phone calls, staff meetings, youth service, youth events on weekends, our college service, college ministry events, set-up, clean up, lunch breaks, and bathroom breaks. Of course I didn't just record the traditional work day. I recorded every minute that a late night crisis phone call came in from a parent or student or a college student who dropped in at our house. Let's just say the folder I slid into their box on Wednesday afternoon was comprehensive.

After three weeks of this play-by-play recording of my ministry the board sent Todd (remember the nice one?) to tell me that enough was enough and that they didn't need the folder anymore. Apparently they had a clearer understanding "what they paid me for." It was to no avail, however. The tone in the board room was continually tense. They weren't willing to acknowledge what God was doing in any part of the church. Not knowing at the time how to describe the environment, I now would have described it as continually awkward and oppressive. Seeing now the dysfunction with the church board without any signs that things would change, we began to pray and look for a ministry role elsewhere.

That "elsewhere" ended up being Phoenix, AZ. The year prior to our departure, Erin and I had met a couple of new friends that were traveling and ministering to the next generation at churches, camps, and retreats through music, comedic skits and preaching. As we began to pray about our future, the Lord brought back to mind this ministry. We soon were on the phone with them and it turned out they were in transition too; looking for someone to fill a needed position. We sensed God was in this, and we made the leap. As we pulled out of town in the U-Haul and our car in tow I remember thinking, "Anything will be better than our current situation." Little did I know what was ahead.

ARIZONA

After rolling through the majestic warm, pink desert of New Mexico our swaying U-Haul hit the Arizona state line. We were thrilled to be joining a creative team of people that believed creativity could be utilized to share Christ's message of love and salvation. The ministry we were joining sat under the leadership covering of a non-denominational church in Scottsdale, AZ. Within just a week after unloading our moving truck, we were on the road traveling full time. We were rarely home because we were booked solid at camps and churches across the country.

The excitement and newness of it all soon wore off as the reality of the daily grind set in. I know that there are many out there who think flying all over the country and staying in hotels would be "the life!" Let me correct you. It isn't. Every hotel room begins to look the same and every meal begins to taste the same. Not to mention our marriage took a continued hit over never being able to be alone with each other.

We were on the road non-stop for about six months when the senior pastor of our home church in Arizona asked us to step into his office. Pastor Jim Cornwall was a towering figure of a man. With bright white hair and a deep voice, you sometimes felt like you were talking to God himself. Pastor Jim had a proposal for Erin and me. The church's current youth pastor was about to leave and move across the country. He asked if we could step in for six months or so and fill in while they looked for a replacement. While we were honored that he would think of us, we were reluctant at first because, after all, we had moved here to be a part of a traveling ministry. However, we also saw it as an opportunity to help our supporting church that was in need as well as get some downtime together as a couple.

Well, to make a long story short, six months turned into three years. The youth ministry took off like a rocket, and we were merely along for the ride. From time to time, I'd step into Pastor Cornwall's office to ask if there was any progress in finding my replacement. "Things are going so well, why would we want to replace you?" he'd say with a smile. It was encouraging to hear, but deep inside I began to recognize an unsettling discontent within me and discouragement.

I soon found myself saying to Erin, "What would you think if we weren't in the ministry anymore?" or "I'm wondering if I should be doing something else with my life." And on and on it went. In the evenings I'd resort to looking at options such as going to medical school or becoming a military pilot (I had served in the military). This went on for months. Finally, one evening over dinner Erin set me straight, "Look, I'll support you in whatever direction you go in life, but I can't continue to ride this rollercoaster blindly of where our life is headed." It was hard to hear, but I needed to hear it.

It was then that I began to go on a prayer journey asking

God to settle in my mind my calling and future. After a few weeks of prayer, the Lord woke me up in the middle of the night and spoke to my spirit, this simple statement, "You are mine. I've set you apart for the preaching of my Word. You are to stop this perpetual hunt for something grander or more exciting." I sat up in bed and began to repent and thank him for the crystal clear clarity he gave me.

With my eyes now opened to the reality of my calling, I began to reevaluate what I was doing and where God was leading. It was around this time that I started to look at the possibility of traveling and speaking again at camps, retreats, and churches. Erin was fully on board, and I began my transition out of the youth pastor role I had held for three years. I immediately felt renewed again at this faith leap in front of me; stepping out of this boat of security onto the white water of trusting God with the future.

For six non-stop months I traveled, preaching around the country at various events and services. I was thrilled.

It definitely was a thrill ride, since our second son, Landon (who wasn't planned) was born. During the holiday season of 2004, scheduling speaking engagements was difficult. Without these engagements we had no income. It was go time. To make ends meet I took on three jobs. I waited tables every night at an Italian restaurant, was a substitute teacher Monday-Friday, and shelved pool chemicals on Saturdays. It was a taxing schedule. I couldn't complain; Erin was at home with a toddler and a newborn.

Erin and I have spoken many times about that season of our lives. We honestly don't know how we made it financially. Each week we gathered up what came in on the kitchen table and laid out what would go to which bills. We always gave 10% back to the Lord right off the top as an act of worship that it was He who had provided everything we had. Somehow there was always enough.

The grueling schedule had some horrendous down sides. Erin and I rarely saw each other, and I was hardly home with the boys. With my schedule at full tilt all the time, I was unable to give the needed time to writing and scheduling speaking engagements. This caused a perpetual cycle of not being able to get back on the road to minister. I had to provide for my family. At some point the pace became unbearable. I remember staggering in after a long Saturday of stocking shelves and waiting tables into the night. As I got ready for bed, I remember telling Erin, "I don't know how much longer I can keep this up." She was supportive, but didn't know of any other options.

It was in this desperate state that I made one of the biggest mistakes in my ministry. I had heard through the grapevine that church planting was taking off in south Texas where I'm from. I got on the phone with some of the representatives of a church fellowship that was helping plant churches. After a few phone interviews I was asked if I wanted to move to North Houston and plant a church. I got off the phone and immediately told Erin I was going on a prayer walk to pray about this opportunity. I was back within thirty minutes and telling Erin to pack her bags, we're going to Houston! Erin was supportive as always, but she'd also tell you now that she was concerned that I was hitting the eject button because I was feeling overwhelmed.

Here's the looking back with 20/20 vision truth: I didn't

hear from God. All I could see was a way out from under the load I was working. We sold our home and were pulling out of our driveway within a month of that phone call. We couldn't believe how fast we were on our way. Our hearts were full of excitement as we looked to the future, but I didn't know then, what I know now; and I want to warn you before you make a blind leap out of shear frustration. No doubt there are times for change and transition in our lives. There's a season for everything, but you must make sure you're not running from something. You can't outrun yourself.

BLAME IT ON TEXAS

Erin and I have always lived by the motto, "Go Big or Go Home." When we commit to something we go chips all in. So it won't surprise you that within a month of being in Houston we had already started construction on our new home. We picked out the spot of our home so that it would be centrally located in the part of the city that we were to be planted. While we waited to meet with district officials to help us get started on the church, I jumped in to find a nine to five job that could support our family as we planted. I took a leap with my uncle Danny in the loan officer business. He was highly competent and extremely patient as he tried to bring this newbie into a basic understanding of how the business worked. But, it was slow going. By slow, I mean I wasn't making a dime. The business is all about networking and I knew no one. Week after week went by without any progress. Both Erin and I began to worry since no money was coming in. We knew we couldn't live on our savings forever.

Adding to some of the hurt and fear during this time was the fact that I lost two of my beloved cousins that were close to my age. My cousin Wes died while sitting on his back patio playing his guitar from what the coroner ruled as an "unknown cause". His heart just stopped. My other cousin, Chris, was killed in an accidental altercation with the police. This pain was compounded by the fact that we had lost his older brother Josh (whom I spent almost every weekend during high school with) to a vehicle accident a few years earlier. It was a brutal time of loss for our entire family.

Then came the kicker. As summer came to a close we finally were able to meet with church fellowship state officials to talk through the needed next steps for our church plant. We were nervous and excited as we met at their central office to talk about the future. That excitement quickly turned to frustration and anger as these leaders told us they had made a mistake. They explained that they had inadvertently given our area to someone else.

"I'm sorry. What?" I fumed. Yep, they had already told another individual that they could plant in the same area. "But we sold our home in Arizona, moved here and have now built a house in that area based on your invitation to come and plant!"

It was obvious that a few of the leadership panel were embarrassed and felt conflicted. The rest seemed not to be bothered in the slightest. After some awkward silence and some strained invitations for us "look at other options in other cities", Erin and I made our way to the car. You could have cut the tension with a knife as we drove out of the parking lot.

I'll spare you some of the declarations that were made as we drove home that afternoon, but needless to say we were both irate and hurt beyond measure.

With a commission only job that wasn't paying a dime and a mortgage payment now due on a house that was built in the wrong city, our emotional tanks dipped to a new low. Nothing seemed to be working; not my job, not our original plan to plant a church, and not even our marriage. The constant stress seemed to bring out the worst in our relationship. The stress Erin was dealing with as she cared for our two little ones compounded as she watched me leave every day for a job that wasn't contributing anything to our family. Tension was mounting in our marriage in a hurry. We grew distant from one another and found out quickly that while we certainly loved each other, we didn't like each other all that much.

My walk with the Lord grew cold. We had found a local church to attend, but to me it was a constant reminder of what had been taken from me. I wasn't praying. I wasn't reading my Bible. I was frustrated, angry, and bitter.

I began to feel like a loser husband, father, and pastor. After a couple of weeks of licking my wounds I reached out to my best friend from high school, Rob Rucker who also lived in Houston. I let him know that I was on the hunt for a job that actually paid money. He immediately told me about an opening at his company. It was a job that required good public speaking and people skills giving orientations to companies being on-boarded with our company's services. The best part was that they were looking to hire immediately. "This sounds like a job made for me," I told Erin as I got off the phone. "I can do that!"

I sent my resume in before the opening even made it to the job board of the company. Within a week I was interviewed and hired. The job seemed to be an answer to prayer. Finally, something had gone our way. The downside of the job was that it required an extensive amount of travel. I had brushed this aside when I interviewed for the job, initially, because I was so desperate to find work. I didn't realize that I was setting our family up for unneeded pain.

My skill level for the corporate job fit great, but I was immediately traveling a ton. Three to four days a week away wasn't unheard of. I thought having actual income would lighten the stress on our marriage, but my time away only seemed to compound it. While Erin appreciated my work to provide, she also began to resent the fact that I was away too much. I began to resent her resentment and thus a vicious cycle began.

Our marriage had begun to feel like we were simply roommates. Conversations that mattered weren't being had. It was all surface. There were no date nights. Intimacy grew stale. We had become merely roommates. Our two boys who were toddlers at the time got little time from me. I was consumed with work and stopped giving them needed attention they deserved.

Our marriage had sunk to a place I never thought it would go: cold, distant, and hurting. Unbelievably, I was even entertaining thoughts of separation. In the middle of my fear, discouragement, and failure I had let my heart get twisted and was seriously looking over the cliff of my life thinking things might be better elsewhere. I truly felt like my dreams and my calling had died.

But God stepped in.

In the middle of this crisis, God opened my eyes to what

He had given me. Erin and I jumped in to counseling and began the long, arduous journey of healing. I began the transformation of becoming the Dad my sons deserved. My prayer time came alive, and I was hearing the voice of the Lord again.

It was about six months later that we found ourselves in that McDonald's I wrote of at the start; with fries flying and Erin unknowingly unlocking my chains with, "Don't you think it's time you go back to doing what you were called to do. I think it's time for us to move forward."

Perhaps you need to hear those same words: it's time to move forward.

My prayer is that you'll take hold of this journey to find forward movement again in your life. While this chapter was all about me. The remaining chapters are all about you and what God longs to do in your life, and I've been praying for just that.

CHAPTER 2

FEAR VS. FAITH

Men are not afraid of things, but of how they view them.

—Epictetus

Dropping ten thousand feet faster than my stomach could handle, I gripped the arm rests of my seat and looked up to my mom with both a question and declaration, "Are we going to die?" and "I think I'm going to throw . . ." My mother's intuition had already kicked in and before I knew it my head was being shoved into an airline vomit bag. (She definitely earned her mother's pay that night).

We were on a red eye flight from California to Texas when we ran smack dab into a massive thunderstorm and were tossed around like my dog Sarge's play toy. Though I was only seven at the time I clearly remember my mom squeezing my hand (cutting off the circulation) as she looked up and prayed, "God please don't let us die." (I don't recommend saying this audibly in front of your kids. It doesn't calm a kid down.) However, the immediate benefit was that I began to pray along with her, believing that if we teamed up we were bound to get a faster response from the Lord. We must have gotten through because we soon safely landed with a collective applause from all passengers and me asking my mom to loose the death grip she had on my hand.

I pray that you don't ever have to endure a storm like that in a plane, but we do have to recognize that the storms of life's circumstances are normal. We can't stick our head in the sand acting like life isn't hard, it just plain is. It's with this in mind that I want us to look at two different storms found in scripture that I believe can shed some light on how we should perceive our own personal storms, view God, and how we should respond in the midst of them.

Let me take you to the gospel of Mark as he gives an account of a very real storm that Jesus and his disciples faced at the height of his ministry. Jesus has just gotten through with a full day of ministry and he's exhausted and in need of rest. Let's drop into this story:

Mark 4:35–41:

On that day, when evening had come, he said to them, "Let us go across to the other side." And leaving the crowd, they took him with them in the boat, just as he was. And other boats were with him. And a great windstorm arose, and the waves were breaking into the boat, so that the boat was already filling. But he was in the stern, asleep on the cushion. And they woke him and said to him, "Teacher, do you not care that we are perishing?" And he awoke and rebuked the wind and said to the sea, "Peace! Be still!" And the wind ceased, and there was a great calm. He said to them, "Why are you so afraid? Have you still no faith?" And they were filled with great fear and said to one another, "Who then is this, that even the wind and the sea obey him?"

It's easy to read passages like these and fail to put ourselves in the boat with them, but I want you to climb into the fishing boat with these men. As they cross the sea, a squall kicks up, and this nasty storm begins to bombard the boat. Do you feel the spray of the sea on your face and the raging wind they were sailing into? They're taking on water, and these guys truly believe without exaggeration that they're going to die.

They go to Jesus who is asleep at the back of the boat. They wake him and say, "We're about to die. Don't you know what's going on? Don't you care?" Jesus gets up, and commands the wind and the waves, "Peace! Be still!" Immediately there's "great calm", Mark writes. I imagine water like glass in this moment.

The disciple's reaction to this divine meteorological miracle is one of Holy fear, "Who is he that even the wind and waves obey his words?" Now, right here is where many stop with this story. We're amazed at the power that Jesus displays over the weather. (And we should be.)

However, I want you to notice something. There is no indication that Jesus was even going to get up from his nap. The disciples go and wake him, and he does what he has to do to calm them down, but we see no indication Jesus was going to get up.

He doesn't wake up and feel disoriented and yell, "Whoa!

21

What's going on? Why didn't you guys wake me sooner? We have to do something! Let's figure this out!"

No. He gets up and says, "Peace! Be Still!" It is then that he goes on to chastise them for not believing they would make it.

It seems Jesus is less concerned about the wind and the waves, and more concerned about the disciple's lack of faith. We don't get a picture that he's panicking, "Oh my word! Guys, you have to wake me up sooner when things like this happen!" Does Jesus mean that the disciples should have sat in the boat and done nothing? No, that would have been silly.

Imagine when Jesus told them, "let's go across to the other side", if the disciples would have just sat in the boat and waited, maybe even began to pray, but never actually began to sail. What do you think Jesus' reaction would have been? Jesus might wake up and notice that they're just sitting there, "What are you doing, why aren't we moving? And the disciples reply: "Well, we're praying our way over!" No, there's an obedience and a rowing to our faith!

I was reminded of this lesson God taught me a few years ago as I was on a prayer walk on our church property. Our church sits on sixty-two acres in the woods, so there is plenty of room to roam. As I walked up our long church driveway, I stopped and looked at our church sign near the road and God clearly spoke to me these words, "Pull up those weeds under the sign."

Odd. I know.

It was clearly the Holy Spirit speaking. I walked over and began to pull weeds all the while saying out loud, "Why do I need to pull weeds? I'm out here to pray. This is why we use weed killer." I began to think that maybe this would be one of those miraculous moments that because I was out here pulling weeds someone would drive by and say, "God told me you'd be here" or something.

Nope.

God said, "Pull." Another few minutes went by as I grappled with the wild onions in the soil when all of a sudden He spoke to me these words, "It's been a long time since you've obeyed me with something this small. Nathan, I don't just want your obedience on the things you perceive as a big deal: ministry, family, the big do's and don'ts. I want it all. Obedience is better than sacrifice."

I kneeled there on the ground for a few moments hit hard by the truth. I prayed, "Lord, I'm yours." He said, "Now, you can go pray." I listened and obeyed. Upon reflection I was reminded that we, many times, miss out on great miracles that God desires to do in and through us because we don't obey the smaller steps that lead to those miracles. There might be small tasks, but there's no such thing as small obedience. When God says pull weeds . . . pull. When God says to row your boat, you row.

Strong faith works the sails and steers the rudder of our life as needed; with a faith that Jesus is going to get us to the other side. Strong faith works hard with the gifts, resources, and wisdom God's given us, has the tough conversations, goes through treatment and procedures . . . knowing that He's going to walk us through it all.

It is in Him sustaining us through our storms (when others are washing out, and shipwrecking their faith), when we're walking through the valley of the shadow of death and know

He's with us that our faith is maturing. Look again at Jesus' response to the disciples, you get the feeling Jesus is expressing, "Guys, you still don't have faith in me? I'm in the boat with you!"

While there wasn't an abundance of faith in the boat, there was plenty of fear and that was the problem. Our spiritual progress is halted when we allow fear to lead instead of faith. We all know what it's like when all of a sudden we get caught in a fearful moment, when we're freaked out about the future, about a sudden crisis that pounces upon us, about our health or the health of another, about how that job situation is going to work out, our finances, the list goes on. We can all relate.

 Our spiritual progress is halted when we allow fear to lead instead of faith.

It reminds me of the man who goes to visit his doctor for some test results. The doctor walks in and says, "Well, Mike, I have some bad news, and I have worse news." Mike says, "Hit me with it Doc." The Doctor leans in and says, "The bad news is you have twenty-four hours to live." "What could be worse than that?" the man replies. The doctor sighs and says, "I forgot to tell you yesterday."

That's bad news and a bad joke.

This is the kind of bad news the disciples were facing in their hearts and minds during this storm, but Jesus points out that the remedy is faith in Him. Consider this: had they had faith in the midst of the storm, the miracle would not have been needed. They would have made it across because that's where Jesus said they were going.

Jesus didn't say, "We're going to start across but end up in a storm, capsize and then sink." No, he said, "Let us go to the other side." We must cling to God's promised word!

When it comes to the storms we face, God can certainly remove it, but more often He chooses to take us through it. Yet, many of us would rather have the miracle without the storm. Like the disciples, we'd rather God rescue us than sustain us. We all want the fix, but what if we've been called to endure and trust Him in the midst of hardship? You can be sure that there are times when God steps to the bow of the boat of our lives and speaks, "Peace, be still." Yet, other times He comes and says, "My peace I give you." God wants us to trust and believe for the miracle, but also trust Him in the midst of our perceived chaos.

In my own life I have to admit that I bring much of this chaos on myself. I am notorious for being forgetful. "Where did I put my wallet, my keys, that book I was reading?" Thankfully my wife Erin has the gift of a photographic memory for where all these items are at any one time. She amazes me. Unfortunately, forgetting inanimate objects are the least of my worries when it comes to forgetting.

Sometimes I forget God is able. Maybe in a moment of struggle or overwhelming stress you've forgotten too. Even as believers we sometimes fail to believe. Listen to this dramatic conversation between Jesus and the father of a child who desperately needed a miracle:

"And Jesus asked his father, 'How long has this been happening to him?' And he said, 'From childhood. And it has often cast him into fire and into water, to destroy him. But if you can do anything, have compassion on us and help us.' And Jesus said to him, 'If you can! All things are possible for one who believes.' Immediately the father of the child cried out and said, 'I believe; help my unbelief'" (Mark 9:21–24)!

"I believe; help my unbelief." That statement alone sums up the faith of many. Many times we believe in a general sense, but don't believe for our own circumstances. If we read on we find that Jesus meets this father's faith where he is and delivers the child. Jesus is kind that way, meeting us where we are. He desires to meet you where you are today as well.

While I can't give you the answers to all of life's hardships, I can tell you why we as followers go through difficult and painful times. It is in the testing of our faith that we become more like Jesus and that's the Father's goal.

CHAPTER 3

THE GIFT IN YOUR STORM

*Trials teach us what we are; they dig up the soil,
and let us see what we are made of.*

—Charles Spurgeon

W hat if the worst thing that has ever happened to you didn't have to be wasted? What if the next time life hit the fan and your life seemed to be unraveling at the seams you could actually have joy in the midst of it all? These "what ifs" don't have to just be speculation. Scripture says this can be a reality. As you read the following passage of scripture keep in mind that James (the brother of Jesus) is writing to Christians who have been facing severe hardship and suffering. Read these verses:

James 1:2–4:

Count it all joy, my brothers, when you meet trials of various kinds, for you know that the testing of your faith produces steadfastness. And let steadfastness have its full effect, that you may be perfect and complete, lacking in nothing.

Notice James doesn't say "if" trials come, but "when." Trials come like the rain and it rains on everyone. Look at the first truth James points toward. He isn't specific about the trials, but what our attitude should be toward them. He writes that our attitude should be marked with joy when it comes to how we view our trials. To "count it all joy" is to choose to view all our trials as a gift from God.

It is in the testing of our faith that we become more like Jesus and that's the Father's goal.

This is radical. It's also where many people get hung up in life. They can begin to see all of their trials only as punishment from God or all of their hardships as having no lasting benefits. Yet, how we view our circumstances is the first major breakthrough we need to have if we're going to not be sidelined and paralyzed by the pain we face in life. Now, I don't want to start quoting Zig Ziglar here . . . you know "Your attitude determines your altitude." But how we view what we face in life matters. Our attitude determines our outcomes.

These aren't just empty Hallmark clichés you're reading. There's a treasure chest full of life change buried in this passage of scripture. You can only count it all joy if you believe and own "that the testing of your faith produces steadfastness."

Testing produces steadfastness. Steadfastness for what? What does steadfastness even mean here?

Steadfast (stĕd'făst', -fəst): loyal to God in the face of trouble and difficulty.

If we will look to Christ as leader and sustainer in the middle of our trials, we'll find Him instilling in us a spiritual backbone of steel that doesn't run or shrink back when things get tough. James is telling us that our trials produce a "with God's help I'm not going anywhere" character trait within us. Don't you want that in your life?

It's confession time; and this seems like a good opportunity to come clean. I have been known to have a bit of a heavy foot. I've been pulled over a few times for speeding. I say "few" because it keeps me from having to tell you the exact number. So you won't be surprised to hear that a couple of years ago, I was leaving football practice with my youngest son, Landon, who at the time was eight years old. We were leaving football practice and on the way back I saw blue lights in my rear view mirror.

Ugh.

If you've ever been pulled over, you know the sick feeling that comes over you. All of a sudden all of these metaphors come to mind as you imagine how your money is being wasted: maybe it's your money being flushed down the toilet or your cash going up in flames. It stinks. And of course you're calculating how your insurance premium will go up (as the insurance agents reading nod). It's not a good feeling.

Back to my story.

After seeing the lights, I complied like a good citizen and pulled over to the side of the road. My son, who was in the back seat, looked back seeing the lights. He said, "Dad, are they going to arrest you?" "I hope not, buddy, because I don't think you can drive this car home." Well, the police officer comes up to the window, and he begins to do the normal thing, "Can I see your license, registration?"

I imagined in the moment, "Oh, did I accidentally give you my church business card? I'm sorry. Let me get my license . . ."

You know, you're willing to try anything! I gave him what he needed and he headed back to his cruiser. As he did I'm thinking, "Come on. Please! How about a warning? Help, help, Lord!" You've been there, calling out to the Lord for mercy!

So Landon and I sat there as he's running my information for what seemed like forever. Finally, exasperated I said, "What is going on? We're just sitting here!" My son, without missing a beat from the back of the car, (taking some excerpt from one of the many lectures of mine), said, "Dad, sometimes we just need to sit and think about what we've done."

"Are you kidding me?" I replied. "Thank you, Son. I feel so much better now. Have you thought about writing greeting cards for a living?"

After a few minutes the officer came back and gave me a ticket. I had learned my lesson, never get a ticket when your son is in the car! Imagine, though, if after I got my ticket that I just sat there and never drove again, never moving on. Sadly, this is true for many in their lives. How many of us know others that have been in the faith, but when life has hit the fan they've bailed. This is what happened to me ten years ago when the church plant didn't happen and when my marriage was on the rocks. I allowed my circumstances to dictate my view of God instead of allowing my view of God to dictate how I viewed my circumstances.

God's testing in your life is always about giving; instilling in you the character of Jesus. If you're like me, maybe you've prayed many times: "Lord, I want to grow and mature in my faith." Well, one of the crucial elements of maturing as a Christian is enduring testing and life's challenges. Someone that has not endured testing and challenges cannot mature. Notice the period there. Life isn't a thirty minute sitcom where everything is resolved in a half hour. There are no secret pills or formulas to be found in a book to "get" maturity.

The Lord uses what we must endure here to mature and perfect us into a person of God that will bring Him the most glory. That should be our prayer. James is saying if we'll view trials this way as a gift from God to grow us from an immature believer to a mature believer, we really can count it all joy!

Let me be clear. This isn't a joy that looks forward to pain, heartache and frustration. Rather, it is a mindset that views trials as a gift that brings about something glorious. C. S. Lewis pointed to this truth when he compared this transformation to a house renovation:

> Imagine yourself as a living house. God comes in to rebuild that house. At first, perhaps, you can understand what He is doing. He is getting the drains right and stopping the leaks in the roof and so on; you knew that those jobs needed doing and so you are not surprised. But presently he starts knocking the

house about in a way that hurts abominably and does not seem to make any sense. What on earth is he up to? The explanation is that he is building quite a different house from the one you thought of – throwing out a new wing here, putting on an extra floor there, running up towers, making courtyards. You thought you were being made into a decent little cottage: but he is building a palace. He intends to come and live in it himself.[1]

God brings us to life through trial. He hones our character. He makes us more like Him. The house must be demolished in order for us to be perfected and be like Christ. The house can't just have a new coat of paint or some plaster on the walls. Walls will be torn down. Additions made.

That means: family tragedy = not wasted
past abuse = not wasted
maligned for your faith = not wasted
cancer = not wasted
relationship strain = not wasted
financial hardship = not wasted . . . you get the idea.

Here's the bottom line: The path to maturity runs through trials. Obstacles in this life don't have to be wasted, they can be one of the tools that make you into the man or woman of God He's designed you to be. We can't escape trials in life, so why not embrace all God has for us in them?

Read the Apostle Paul's encouragement regarding this shaping that God is doing in us; God shapes us if we allow him:

Philippians 1:6:

And I am sure of this, that he who began a good work in you will bring it to completion at the day of Jesus Christ.

Philippians 2:12–13:

Therefore, my beloved, as you have always obeyed, so now, not only as in my presence but much more in my absence, work out your own salvation with fear and trembling, for it is God who works in you, both to will and to work for his good pleasure.

Let me say this again: There is only one way for his this "work" to take place in us; testing and trial.

 We can't escape trials in life, so why not embrace all God has for us in them?

I'd like you to think about that test or trial you are walking through, right now. If you can't immediately put your finger on it, you can figure it out quickly by thinking about the issue you absolutely wish didn't exist. That thing you wish you could go around, go under, just avoid completely.

No matter what you are walking through right now, there is hope and joy in the fact that God is working things out in us for His good pleasure.

My mom is a *huge* William Shatner fan. As a kid I remember her watching *Star Trek* every night it was on, and I was left to endure Captain Kirk's reflective monologues on a regular basis. The only highlight of the show for me was when the crew was "beamed" anywhere. You remember, they were teleported down to a new planet and then back to their ship. I was amazed by the idea of being able to just show up somewhere without having to take the time or the effort to actually make the trip.

My life balloon was deflated at the age of seven when I was told that no, you can't actually be "beamed" up or out or anywhere. Still, I think the frustration still lingers for many of us that want to go somewhere without having to take the necessary steps to get there.

We want a shortcut; an easy button. We want to play without having to pay. We want a deeper walk with Jesus, but not have to invest the time with Him. We want to be a writer, without the work. We want to lead without having to learn. We want to go global with our faith without having to go across the street: (Insert your desired short-cut here.)

Sometimes this comes from just plain laziness. Other times it comes from this reoccurring enemy that we've already mentioned: fear.

There could be a million combinations of why we're not embracing the process where God wants to lead us: to the journey through adversity. But here's a not-so-well kept secret: if we got our wish to avoid "the work" we'd be miserable. Why? You'd have no story to tell.

An ending is only as interesting as the story that takes you there. Our lives are no different. The challenges, the effort, the work, the process, it's all the adventure. That's the good stuff in the middle of our story. To avoid it would mean you could never mentor, never be able to reach back for a much needed overcoming moment in your story for the encouragement to endure your present, to encourage another. The "becoming" doesn't happen when you arrive, it happens in the journey; in your story. There is no easy button. There is no way around the hard stuff. It's part of you becoming.

James goes on to write:

James 1:4:
And let steadfastness have its full effect, that you may be perfect and complete, lacking in nothing.

Again, this reinforces the idea that without enduring trial and maturing through it we will be lacking something that God intends. We're in desperate need of trials to produce the man or woman of God. In all of this the Father desires to shape us, not only act like Jesus, but also react like Jesus in our suffering. One that trusts Him when life doesn't seem to go our way.

Can I push pause for a moment?

The word "legacy" gets thrown around a lot these days. People have an innate desire to be remembered. Not just remembered, but remembered well. We want to leave something behind us that lasts. I see and hear this most when I'm around those that have lost a loved one.

When we experience this type of loss in our lives we're struck with our mortality. Our eyes are opened and we're stopped dead in our tracks. As a pastor I've watched countless people at funerals stare with moist eyes at the casket or urn at the front of the room. Many of them are thinking the same thing, "One day that's going to be me."

When our family and friends step up to the microphone at our funeral we want the words to be rich and have depth. We all want our life to have mattered. We all want to leave a life changing legacy.

But, let me be painfully honest with you; that's too small of a goal. It falls fantastically short of where we should be aiming.

Think about this. I'm willing to bet . . . well, not bet. I'm willing to guess that you most likely know very little about either of your Great Great Grandfathers. I know I don't. You might know where they were born or what ancestral line they came from, but you most likely don't know what kind of man he was. You don't know his small and large accomplishments in life or his life long held values or the type of parent he was. Why? Because most people's legacies are forgotten. Why? Because they slowly fade away as those closest to us fade away. Not only can they be forgotten, they can be misinterpreted. Over time, without the context of our lives and times, our actions can be misunderstood.

So, while a noble legacy is admirable it's not the pinnacle of life. The highest aim of our lives should be pleasing and bringing glory to our Creator God. It is He that we will stand before to give an account of our lives. I long to hear these defining words from the one who defines our purpose: "Well done my good and faithful servant." To get to that moment will require an endurance and faithfulness through life's difficulties. There's no way around it.

As I write this, my mind is flooded with a catalog of life's storms that God has used to continue to shape me into the man he desires. Some storms were not of my making:

the sexual abuse from a teacher in 3rd grade, growing up in a broken home, a painful start to pastoral ministry with hurt and betrayal.

Then there were trials I brought on myself. I backed up a semi-load of issues and insecurities and unloaded them on my marriage. In my early years of ministry I had a tendency to get distracted and get ahead of what God was doing in my life and thus brought more pain and frustration on myself, my wife, and I'm sure, many others. The list goes on.

Yet, in it all God was shaping me and He'll do that consistently in your life if you'll allow Him. Obstacles in this life don't have to be wasted, they can be one of the tools that make you into the man or woman of God He's designed you to be. Believe it.

Will you allow the Holy Spirit to change your view of your trials and see them as a tool of God to produce in you a mature follower of Jesus?

CHAPTER 4

SHINING IN YOUR STORM

*We could never learn to be brave and patient
if there were only joy in the world.*

—Hellen Keller

As I stood at the edge of the boat holding Erin's hand I thought to myself, "what are we about to do?" It was the last day of our honeymoon, and we were wrapping up our last day in Nassau, Bahamas. We had made a quick jaunt across the bay and had caught a ferry back to the main pier when a light storm began to pick up on the bay. The small boat we were in began to rise and fall quickly with every swell.

The captain of the small vessel, for some strange reason, decided not to go back to the original pier we had left from, but take a shortcut to the much higher concrete cruise ship pier. At the height of the swells the side of the boat was even with the taller pier, when it fell, there was a six foot difference.

One of the boat engineers motioned Erin and I to come to the back of the boat. He wanted us to jump from the boat to the massive pier. There was no tying the ship or making it just right. This was going to be all about timing. If we timed it right, we'd be fine, if we didn't, one or both of us would fall between the boat and the pier and be crushed.

I grabbed Erin's hand and she looked at me with a nervous smile (I guess she was trusting my judgment that this was okay.) Little did she know I was scared out of my mind. The boat engineer insisted as he watched us hesitate. I told Erin, "Here we go: One . . . Two . . . Three." As the boat came up from the bottom of the swell, Erin and I leapt just in time to find ourselves standing (gratefully I might add) on solid ground. It was only later that we stopped and realized what could have happened to us had we missed that jump.

The same is true for our lives, it's only after the storm that we have a clearer perspective. I love one of John Maxwell's famous quotes, "People say that wisdom comes with age, but sometimes age just shows up alone." Most people have no way to see what God is doing and grow in wisdom through their storms of life because they don't take time to prayerfully reflect on their experiences. We live life at such breakneck speed that we don't consider how we're being shaped by God in the middle of it all. Maxwell goes on to explain that it's only upon reflection and evaluation of what we've experienced that we grow in insight and wisdom. If we do this we can truly begin to see the fingerprints of what God is doing in our lives. Having a regular prayer time (time of silence) with the Lord can allow yourself that opportunity to not only look to Jesus, but look inward to see the person you're becoming in Him.

Go with me to read of another storm found in Acts 27:14–26:

> But soon a tempestuous wind, called the north-easter, struck down from the land. And when the ship was caught and could not face the wind, we gave way to it and were driven along. Running under the lee of a small island called Cauda, we managed with difficulty to secure the ship's boat. After hoisting it up, they used supports to undergird the ship. Then, fearing that they would run aground on the Syrtis, they lowered the gear, and thus they were driven along. Since we were violently storm-tossed, they began the next day to jettison the cargo. And on the third day they threw the ship's tackle overboard with their own hands. When neither sun nor stars appeared for many days, and no small tempest lay on us, all hope of our being saved was at last abandoned.
>
> Since they had been without food for a long time, Paul stood up among them and said, "Men, you should have listened to me and not have set sail from Crete and incurred this injury and loss. Yet now I urge you to take heart, for there will be no loss of life among you, but only of the ship. For this very night there stood before me an angel of the God to whom I belong and whom I worship, and he said, 'Do not be afraid, Paul; you must stand before Caesar. And behold, God has granted you all those who sail with you.' So take heart, men, for I have faith in God that

it will be exactly as I have been told. But we must run aground on some island."

The general mood on the boat is, "It's over. We're going down." The only reason you start throwing cargo over (your money maker) is when it becomes all about saving your life. They, like our previous storm tossed shipmates, don't enjoy the same promise. The promise isn't "there'll be no shipwreck. The promise isn't "you won't go hungry." Jesus doesn't calm this storm; no doubt Paul asked him to.

Paul hears from God that no life will be lost, but the ship will be lost. It's going to run aground.

As we read, we see that there's still immense fear felt by those onboard, they haven't eaten in fourteen days. Let's read on:

Acts 27:33–39:

As day was about to dawn, Paul urged them all to take some food, saying, "Today is the fourteenth day that you have continued in suspense and without food, having taken nothing. Therefore I urge you to take some food. For it will give you strength, for not a hair is to perish from the head of any of you." And when he had said these things, he took bread, and giving thanks to God in the presence of all he broke it and began to eat. Then they all were encouraged and ate some food themselves. (We were in all 276 persons in the ship.) And when they had eaten enough, they lightened the ship, throwing out the wheat into the sea.

Now when it was day, they did not recognize the

land, but they noticed a bay with a beach, on which they planned if possible to run the ship ashore.

The ship does run aground and all 276 people survive as God promised. But it certainly can't be seen as the easy way. There was no miracle of the seas and winds being calmed. No property and possessions being saved. At first glance it doesn't seem to be miraculous at all.

However . . . there is a miracle here.

At its darkest hour . . . before dawn. Paul encourages them to eat up. We're going to make it. Paul displays this peace that's stunning. Read this again:

Acts 27:35:

And when he had said these things, he took bread, and giving thanks to God in the presence of all he broke it and began to eat. Then they all were encouraged and ate some food themselves.

Now, the food was always there. That's not remarkable. The miracle is found in Paul's assured confidence and displayed peace in God as he points to Christ by administering communion amid those aboard the ship. Those aboard watching and listening were encouraged by this: "Maybe WE ARE going to make it!"

God used this storm, loss, and suffering to highlight His existence through Paul who is enduring this suffering as well. Anyone can be perceived as peaceful in peaceful times, but put a man or woman under stress and suffering and you find out quickly what's inside them. Anyone can shine during prosperity,

maturity shines during adversity by moving forward. You shine
and are unstoppable when you walk in the peace of God.

I watched this truth come to life in a man by the name of
Stan Maxwell. I was in my first few weeks of a new pastorate
when Stan approached me after a Sunday message with his
arms outstretched ready to take me into his trademarked bear
hug. After hugging me, he pushed me back, still holding me
on the shoulders and said with toothy grin, "We need to talk.
You need to hear what God has done for me. I'm a walking a
miracle!" We sat down on some chairs nearby and he began
to share some of his life story: his Christian upbringing, his
service in the Marine Corp, his slide into drug addiction, him
coming back to a faith in Christ and being set free from that
addiction, and finally his cancer diagnosis.

 **Anyone can shine during prosperity, maturity
shines during adversity by moving forward.**

The cancer diagnosis hit him like a Mac truck. He had
been enjoying life with his wife, Tracey, and watching his
successful home interior trim business thrive. Now, he had a
new war to fight: there'd be chemo treatments, endless doctor
visits, fatigue, frustration and days when he didn't even want
to get out of bed. But today, Stan was riding high after his
cancer was declared in remission. He felt strongly that God
had healed him completely and wanted to tell the world.

He did just that, a couple of weeks later I found myself
interviewing Stan on camera as he shared much of his story.
The interview was a great encouragement to many as he shared

that cancer had given him clarity and a passion to get up every day and bring God glory with his life, with cancer or without.

About a year later I got a phone call in the early evening. It was Stan. He had just received news that the cancer was back. He no doubt was discouraged, but said, "Time to get back in the fight!" That's exactly what he did as he endured more chemo therapy, experimental drug trials, you name it, he endured it. All the while we prayed and trusted God for his designed healing.

There were some hard days and nights when his body and emotions were pushed to their limits. His wife Tracey walked with him every step of the way. Yet, Stan kept looking up; trusting the Lord for his best. Stan called me the day when doctors looked at Stan and said they'd done all they could do. When I asked him what he was thinking and feeling he said, "I'm at peace."

It was that same peace that spoke loudly to Stan's friends and family that didn't know the Lord. I remember many remarking to me as we stood around his bed in his final hours, "His faith is inspiring" and "I hope I can hold onto God like Stan". Before he closed his eyes for the last time Stan said, "I'm good. God's been good to me. I'm ready to go home."

Stan died in February of 2013. Yet, his clinging faith to God was unstoppable. Throngs of people filed in to our church to celebrate his life and hear of Stan's faith in Christ. Many made decisions to follow Christ after watching Stan's battle and his response in the midst of it all.

Whether your desired miracle takes place: that crisis resolved, that physical healing needed, that relationship restored . . . more than any other circumstance you and I might face,

God is more concerned in what He's doing in and through you than what he can pull you out of.

Go with me to another recorded encounter Jesus has with a young rich ruler. The young man comes and tells Jesus that he wants to follow him, but it's clear that after the discussion Jesus has with him that He's unwilling to leave his wealth behind.

Jesus turns to his disciples and says,

Matthew 19:24–26:

Again I tell you, it is easier for a camel to go through the eye of a needle than for a rich person to enter the kingdom of God." When the disciples heard this, they were greatly astonished, saying, "Who then can be saved?" But Jesus looked at them and said, "With man this is impossible, but with God all things are possible.

Do this for me, look at this verse again.

Matthew 19:26:

. . . With man this is impossible, but with God all things are possible.

You absolutely need to add this verse to your list and branded on your heart. Put this verse in your head, your car, your bathroom, a tattoo . . . whatever. It's that important. We need to remember that God can do the impossible in our lives.

 God is more concerned in what He's doing in and through you than what he can pull you out of.

But notice in this instance Jesus points to His "all things are possible" power toward His saving, life transforming power. To illustrate this point, let me point you to a name you most likely don't know, but should, Horatio Spafford:

Horatio Spafford had known peaceful and happy days as a successful attorney in Chicago. He was the father of four daughters, an active member of the Presbyterian Church, and a loyal friend and supporter of D. L. Moody and other evangelical leaders of his day. Then, a series of calamities began, starting with the great Chicago fire of 1871, which wiped out the family's extensive real estate investments. When Mr. Moody and his music associate, Ira Sankey, left for Great Britain for an evangelistic campaign, Spafford decided to lift the spirits of his family by taking them on a vacation to Europe. He also planned to assist in the Moody-Sankey meetings there.

In November, 1873, Spafford was detained by urgent business, but he sent his wife and four daughters as scheduled on the S.S. Ville du Harve, planning to join them soon. Halfway across the Atlantic, the ship was struck by an English vessel and sank in twelve minutes. All four of the Spafford daughters—Tanetta, Maggie, Annie and Bessie—were among the 226 who drowned. Mrs. Spafford was among the few who were miraculously saved.

Horatio Spafford stood hour after hour on the deck of the ship carrying him to rejoin his sorrowing wife in Cardiff, Wales. When the ship passed the approximate place where his precious daughters had drowned, Spafford received sustaining comfort from God that enabled him to write, "When sorrows like sea billows roll . . . It is well with my soul.[1]

The greatest miracle of this story isn't the amazing timeless hymn that Horatio penned or the thousands upon thousands of people that have been comforted, encouraged and ministered to by it. What strikes me most is that he was able to say in the middle of absolute horrific sorrow, "it is well with my soul." Only God can do that.

Think about your storm. What if the greatest miracle God ever performs in your life is in your spiritual transformation? What if God uses your darkest hour of suffering to bring Him the most glory? What if your story of coming out of that storm in life is exactly what someone needs to hear for them to see Jesus as the light in their own storm?

CHAPTER 5

THE GREATEST LIAR IN THE WORLD

*Worry does not empty tomorrow of its sorrow,
it empties today of its strength.*

—Corrie Ten Boom

It's the thing I have to beat back with a stick every day. I mean every day. If I let this beast take hold I would attempt nothing, risk nothing, and have nothing. I've never met a person who hasn't looked it in the eye.

The villain is worry.

A while back our church kicked off a two weekend push to invite guests to our church and hear the gospel. The two fears I battled with: What if people don't come? What if they don't respond?

Turns out people did come and people did respond. But, I was still left with the question, where does this junk come from? Answer: It comes from fear.

If I could mic up my mind this is what you might hear:

"If people don't invite people, what does that say about my leadership? If people don't respond to the gospel when I preach, what does that say about my preaching? Can I even do this?"

Have you noticed that much of your thinking is dominated by the word "if". Now, that's not always a bad thing. The word "if" is powerful. It's all about potential. But, when we're walking in fear and worry, our "if" is fixated on the potential of failure. When I am walking in faith, the "ifs" turn into seeing the God-potential in my life.

Also, notice another theme throughout my mind conversation, the word "I". This is pride. Most of the time this fear is less about the mission failing and more about me looking like a failure. "What will people think of me if this doesn't work?"

If we let fear and worry run rampant in our lives we'll end up never trying or risking anything. Our motto will end up being, "Never try, never fail." We might not ever have to deal with the pain of failure, but we'll end up suffocating the growth in ourselves and others that we lead. That is failure.

So what's the remedy? On a daily basis I have to drag my pride and worry to the cross and nail it there. God has called me to do the right things for the right reasons and leave the results up to Him. That puts faith over fear and worry in my life.

A specific moment sticks out in my mind when worry was robbing me of every bit of peace I had. I was hanging out with my sons right before bed. I was sitting with my youngest son when I realized he'd been talking to me for a few minutes and I hadn't heard a word. I was completely lost in thought. I take that back; I was lost in worry. Frustrated and a bit embarrassed, I wrapped my arms around my son and hugged him.

As I laid down that night I realized that I'd been giving worry way too much space in my life. I was wrapping up my first year as a senior pastor and my stress level was through the roof. The church had been facing ongoing financial struggles, and I had convinced myself that everything was going to crash and burn around me and that I'd be seen as the person who finally put the church into the ground. My pastoral career would be over forever. After all, who would want a pastor that couldn't lead his church to financial prosperity! I had created my own worst nightmare and was taking every opportunity to replay it myself, sometimes multiple times a day. Yet, as I laid down in prayer that night, God was able to convince me of this truth: Worry is the greatest liar.

Have you ever noticed that rarely anything we worry about ever actually happens? Worry stirs up worst case scenarios in our minds that never seem to materialize. Worry takes the fear of the unknowns of tomorrow and brings them to today. Worry is like the boy who cried wolf, always sounding the alarm, always using fear to get our attention.

Think about this: Would you believe a person that never gave you accurate information? If they were always filling your ear with lies? No . . . you wouldn't because you couldn't trust them. In the same way worry has zero credibility because worry lies and exaggerates.

"This will never come together."

"You're on your own."

"They won't understand."

"We'll never have enough to make it."

Jesus knows the hold anxiety can have on us. That's why he taught us this:

Matthew 6:33–34

But seek first the kingdom of God and his righteousness, and all these things will be added to you. "Therefore do not worry about tomorrow, for tomorrow has enough worry for itself. Sufficient for the day is its own trouble."

Jesus is saying, "Worry is going to come calling daily. You just focus on me and the mission I've given you in this life and I'll take care of you." The problem is that we tend to fall into worry when we're about seeking to build our own kingdom, but when we focus on his kingdom we're reminded that the Lord is covering every bill that comes up.

 While our worries conjure up our worst fears, faith in Christ conquers them.

While our worries conjure up our worst fears, faith in Christ conquers them. Instead of letting your thoughts of worry work you over one more time, kick worry in the teeth. Call worry a liar and move forward with Christ. Start speaking God's truth for your life to those reoccurring worries. Remember, you're not being a "realist" when you give attention to fear. Walk in wisdom and think through what wisdom calls for. But, don't give worry an inch in your life.

THE WAITING ROOM

My family loves road trips. We love being able to get away even if it's for just a day trip. A couple of years ago I put together a special "guys only" trip with my two sons who at the time were eight and nine. They were stoked as we pulled in to a hotel near the beach. We had a plan of hanging out at the hotel pool, enjoying some pizza and hitting the beach the next day. It was going to be an epic weekend! We had just checked in to our room and were just about to throw our swimsuits on when my phone started vibrating repeatedly on the desk as a flurry of text messages from various people came in. They were letting me know that Brandon had died.

Brandon was a vibrant ball of energy that loved the Lord and had endured the ups and downs of a risky heart transplant. Out of high school and pursuing a breakthrough in the music industry, Brandon had big plans. After initially responding well to his new heart, Brandon began to experience complications that in the end were insurmountable by modern medicine. Getting that call left me heartbroken for his family and friends. I sat on the edge of one of the hotel beds as my boys jumped on the beds oblivious to what just happened. I broke the news to the boys that we'd have to come back next week. I grabbed our bag, and we jumped back in the car headed for home to be with Brandon's family and friends.

As I waited in the hospital waiting room to see the family, this truth washed over me: it's hard to wait on God when life hits the fan. I've waited in emergency and surgical waiting rooms when lives were hanging in the balance. I've waited for phone calls in the middle of the night to find out how it all turned out. I've waited for decisions that were being made by others that impacted my future. I've waited with others when they were praying for a breakthrough for their spouse or child. I know what it is to wait on God to do the impossible.

If some of the most difficult moments in life have to do with waiting on God, it would seem that we need to learn how to do it well. This chapter is about doing just that. The Psalmist, King David, gives us this picture of being rescued in the midst of his distress.

Psalm 40:1

I waited patiently for the Lord; he turned to me and heard my cry. He lifted me out of the slimy pit, out of the mud and mire; he set my feet on a rock and gave me a firm place to stand.

Even in these few short verses we find simple, but still rock solid truths for us to cling to:

God knows where you are. Your situation is not unknown to Him. He knows exactly what you're walking through.

Just because you can't see or hear God, doesn't mean he can't see or hear you. Like a toddler in a retail store who wanders behind the clothes on a clothing rack and asks, "Daddy, where did you go?" we tend to believe that He cannot see us. Not true. He's right there.

When we read scripture we find that crying to the Lord is the norm. David wrote, "I waited patiently on the Lord. . . . He heard my cry." Patiently waiting on God doesn't mean there's no crying. I don't know how many times I've gone to sleep in tears while in prayer to the Lord. As I shared earlier, at one point in our marriage, Erin and I were in a place of pain, desperate pain. There were moments when I know we both wondered if there was any hope of us even making it. I shed many tears during those days of the unknown future we both were facing. I'm convinced that crying out to God in the midst of our waiting in the Pit keeps us dependent on the Lord. It's actually when we stop crying out to God that we should be concerned.

Listen to David a few verses later:

Psalm 40:17

But as for me, I am poor and needy; may the Lord think of me, You are my help and my deliverer; you are my God, do not delay.

In difficulty we can easily forget God's track record of deliverance in our lives. That's why we must proactively remind ourselves of this truth.

In the waiting David reminds himself of two pillars of truth:

1. **Who we are:** David reminded himself that he was "poor and needy." Here's a great reminder for us to stay humble and dependent on the Lord.
2. **Who God is:** "my help and deliverer." Grow your faith by reminding yourself of God's faithfulness.

When you're in this place of worry it's a good time to pull out a piece of paper and begin to dump your heart onto the page of every time God has shown himself faithful in your life. I can promise you from experience that you cannot go through this process and not be reminded that God takes care of His own.

This week I was reflecting on this well known passage,

"Trust in the Lord with all your heart, and do not lean on your own understanding. In all your ways acknowledge him, and he will make straight your paths" (Prov. 3:5–6).

Have you considered this idea of trusting God with "all my heart"? This command to trust God with all our heart is crucial in helping us avoid the trap of trusting God with only some or part of our heart. Yet, that's where I live so many times in my walk with the Lord, trusting him with only parts and not the whole.

I'm a huge fan of waffles. My boys are too. They love it when I get up early on a Saturday morning and make Belgian waffles for the family. We pile on the butter and syrup and all of us make sure that each square of the waffle is filled with dripping goodness! (My body thanks me that we only do this every now and then.)

But like the squares on a waffle that hold their own compartment of syrup, we many times compartmentalize the different parts of our lives and separate them from one another: our career, marriage, our children, friendships, finances, health, dreams, the list goes on and on.

When it comes to trusting God we many times choose what compartments we're going to trust him with. We might be okay with trusting him with a majority of them, but we'll keep a select few to carry ourselves. Yet, He calls us to trust Him with our whole heart, leaving no square unturned.

Think about it this way. Imagine making a beautiful golden waffle and spreading butter and syrup into every square except for one square in the middle and then in that one single square in the middle you spoon in some fresh steaming cow manure. (Disgusting, I know. Stay with me!) Despite the manure being in only one square out of the entire waffle, how excited would you be about diving in to eat? You wouldn't, because that one tainted square keeps you from enjoying the whole waffle. The same is true when it comes to trusting God with our lives. Compartmentalizing and holding back even one area of our life will eventually corrupt the whole. God wants our whole heart not because he's selfish, but because he knows what's best for us.

Let me encourage you to do a spiritual inventory. Pause right now and ask yourself this question: "Is there an area in my life that I continue to rely on my own understanding and strength to manage?" Remember our understanding is brittle and incomplete. That's why God tells us not to lean on it. Trust in the Lord. Give him every area of your life. Give Him the whole waffle.

 God wants our whole heart not because he's selfish, but because he knows what's best for us.

You say, "But what if I'm here because of my own stupid-ity?" God has not stopped being your heavenly Dad just because you're in the Pit because of your choices! Just like an earthly father wouldn't leave his son in a pit, how much more does God the father love you? He hears you. He sees you. Worship Him in the waiting. Trust Him. He's already moving.

———

CHAPTER 6

DISMANTLING DISCOURAGEMENT

*We must accept finite disappointment,
but never lose infinite hope.*

—Martin Luther King Jr.

Have you ever seen someone throw a fit in public? It's not pretty. In chapter one I told you about the day the leadership panel admitted to me that they'd made a mistake and already given our area to another church planter. Well, what I didn't tell you was what happened that afternoon when we got home.

When we got back to the house I let Erin go out so I could go to our neighborhood park and clear my head. The park was heavily wooded and provided some trails for many of my prayer walks. As I started on one of the trails I immediately began to pray, "What is going on? We sold our house, we've now built one, I'm working my tail off with nothing to show for it, and I feel like I'm getting nothing from you . . . !"

This went on for a good ten minutes. Finally, while still on my tirade I unknowingly came upon a clearing in the park as I was raising my hands in the air yelling to God, "What are you doing?!" Surprisingly, I heard back, "Playing basketball!" I opened my eyes to see some young boys holding their ball staring back at me in shock. Needless to say that wasn't the answer I was looking for.

I know what it's like when it feels like your well of hope has run dry. Hope is a precious commodity. When someone feels they've lost it, their life truly feels unbearable. That's why this God-breathed proverb resonates with us all.

Prov. 12:13:

Hope deferred makes the heart sick, but a longing fulfilled is a tree of life.

If you've lived any bit of hardship at all in this life you know what this heart sickness feels like. The weight of hopelessness can at times feel bone crushing. When we're in this place we begin to make statements like, "This will never work out, I'll never make it, no one wants to be my friend. We'll never get out of this hole. No one cares. I can't get this. Nothing ever goes my way. What if this is all there is? I'm just not smart enough, I've tried so many times . . . it's useless, can't I ever catch a break?"

This kind of discouragement can make the heart sick, and we can end up emotionally paralyzed in life and miss out on all that God has for us. Let me also remind you that being sidelined by discouragement doesn't just affect you. It brings a halt to your God ordained ministry that he's given you for your family, friends, and community. This doesn't have to be. With God's help you can end up breaking through discouragement like a freight train.

To do that we're going to need to get real.

There are a million reasons why I love the Bible. One of those reasons is that the Bible is brutally honest. It makes no attempt to sugar coat the mistakes of its heroes. We see countless examples of God openly sharing the dirty laundry of our pillars of faith: Abraham the liar, Moses the murderer, David the adulterer, Peter the coward . . . I could go on and on. How would you like your life's biggest mistake to be sermon material in the best-selling book in the history of mankind? No? I'd pass as well.

Why was God intentional about having these mistakes of our beloved heroes in scripture? Here's three reasons:

1. **To Make Much of His Grace:** Time and time again we see God's grace shown to these men and women after some of life's biggest blow ups. God doesn't ignore their sin. He deals with it head on and then extends amazing grace. This allowed these great leaders to go on to do incredible exploits for His glory. He turns what they meant for evil for good every time. God desires to make much of His grace so that we will make much of his grace.

2. **So We Could Learn From Their Mistakes:** Life's too short to try and learn from just our own failures. We can grow exponentially if we'll choose to learn from the sin of those we find in scripture.

God knows that we can be mentored by the mistakes of others if we'll take heed and learn from those that have gone before us. We must be lifelong students of others.

3. **To Give us Hope:** It's so easy for us to deify the men and women in the Bible and miss the point that they were flesh and bone just like you and me. The apostle Paul wrote that Elijah the prophet was "just a man." When we see these sins recorded in scripture, we're reminded of their humanity and that as they repented of their sin God chose to use them in spite of their failures. Jesus makes this same hope available to anyone that will embrace him as savior and leader of their life. In your heart you should be yelling, "There's hope for me too!"

As we move forward, I want you to embrace the honesty of scripture with a desire to grow. Don't allow the mistakes or vulnerable prayers of your biblical heroes to spin you out. Listen to their counsel. They're teaching us even today if we'll listen.

One of our imperfect heroes was King David. Not only was he not perfect, we have the gift of his written psalms that in many ways act as somewhat of a diary of his spiritual life full of internal defeats and victories. For example, he writes in Psalm 31 a list of discouraging issues that he's walking through himself: the shame of his mistakes, people rejecting him, tearing him down, gossiping about him, and some plotting against him. To top it all off his health is fading because of all this. HE IS STRESSED OUT. At the climax of the passage he writes:

I had said in my alarm, I am cut off from your sight. But you heard the voice of my pleas for mercy when I cried to you for help. Love the Lord, all you his saints! The Lord preserves the faithful but abundantly repays the one who acts in pride. Be strong, and let your heart take courage, all you who wait for the Lord (Psalm 31:22–24).

David writes that "in his alarm" he felt he was cut off from God's sight; that he'd been abandoned by God. Just like I felt when I was yelling in the park while praying. We've all made statements in stressful times to others and to God that upon reflection we would say, "I didn't mean that."

The importance is that we catch ourselves and David does . . . "But you heard the voice of my pleas . . ." He goes on to share what He's learned. David is giving us a gift. He's saying, "Listen . . . learn from me":

Love the Lord, all you his saints! The Lord preserves the faithful but abundantly repays the one who acts in pride. Be strong, and let your heart take courage, all you who wait for the Lord (Psalm 31:23–24).

Who is this counsel to? It's to "all you who wait for the Lord!" All you waiting for an answer, a breakthrough, direction, a resolution, provision, strength, a healing. To you He says be strong! Hold on . . . because even though everything within you wants to collapse, give up, give in, stay home and sleep, withdraw and isolate yourself from family and friends; BE STRONG.

We're going to need the Lord's help to be strong because it takes real strength in God to stand in the midst of adversity. David writes, "let your heart take courage." Sometimes we don't want to let our heart take courage. It's just easier to let our mind go anywhere it pleases. It takes no effort to be fearful and discouraged. No one has to work at being afraid.

I know this better than anyone. Several years ago when I was overseeing multiple next generation pastors at a church, I found myself needing to make some personnel changes. While we were looking for new people to fill these roles, I was leading multiple areas of ministry at one time. Needless to say I was overwhelmed. We didn't seem to be making any progress in our search for these new pastors. I was working longer hours and began to hit a wall of stress and fatigue. One night while venting to my wife about our predicament she said (in an effort to be consoling) "It will all work out."

You would have thought I would have been grateful for her hope filled words. Instead, my stress-filled heart took them as cliché and unhelpful. I shot back, "Really? It's going to work out? Wow, I feel so much better now. I was thinking it wasn't, but now that you've said 'it's all going to work out' I guess it will. What was I thinking? All this time I've been busting my tail trying to figure all of this stuff when I should have known it was 'all going to work out!'"

I know what you're thinking . . . what a jerk.

I agree.

The truth that gripped me wasn't stress. It was fear. Fear that I couldn't lead through this transition. Fear that we wouldn't find the right people. Fear that I would ultimately fail as a leader. I had given fear a backstage-ALL ACCESS pass to my heart and mind. I allowed myself to believe that because nothing had worked out yet, nothing was ever going to work out.

Think for a moment about how haphazardly we allow thoughts in and let them run rampant. Thoughts of fear and negativity are like the mean, negative friend or family member we know that comes over to visit for lunch, but ends up staying for a week. Where did we mess up? Letting them in to begin with.

The first way we let our heart take courage is by dealing with our current way of thinking about God, ourselves and our circumstances. You must refuse to be the one that says to yourself, "this is just who I am and who I'll always be." We think we're being a realist and practical when we think this way, but the truth is we're just being NEGATIVE. Stop giving fear and discouragement a backstage pass to your life.

We teach kids at a young age how to talk to adults and to one another properly. Yet, we need to teach ourselves and the following generations how we should be talking to ourselves.

I'm not talking about shallow statements of "I'm good enough, I'm smart enough, and people like me." This isn't about self-esteem. This is about how God sees me and my circumstance. We must be speaking God's truth to ourselves.

This is crucial if we're going to "let our heart take courage" as David encourages us to do. The first part of "letting our heart take courage" is that we must recognize fearful and destructive thoughts for what they are: dangerous. These thoughts blind us to the reality of what God says about who we are and our current circumstance. They refuse to allow faith and hope to enter the picture. When we aren't led by faith, fear leads the way and it never leads anywhere pretty. Never anywhere better; certainly not to the lush green fields of the Father's presence.

Not only do we need to recognize the damage negative thoughts can bring, we must serve our negative, discouraging thoughts an eviction notice. GET OUT!

CHAPTER 7

GET OFF THE CRAZY TRAIN

True spiritual life depends not on probing our feelings and thoughts from dawn to dusk but on "looking off" to the Savior!

—Watchman Nee

I t was thirty-six hours of absolute torture. The idea of a train trip across America's heartland sounded amazing. I had signed up with my youth group for an inner-city mission's trip to Chicago. We'd be boarding the train in Houston and making our way north. Sounds fun right? Wrong. It was brutal. While there were moments of lush panoramic scenery, the majority of the trip was a nightmare.

Dreams were dashed from the outset. This wasn't a ticket that included a spot in a sleeper car. Nope. It was a single coach seat fare which meant sleep was illusive. Along the way a mechanical issue with another train meant our train was unable to resupply its food stores. The train quickly ran out of food and could only offer a few peanut butter crackers. If that wasn't enough, the main bathroom for our train car stopped working. I'm sure the city of Chicago could smell us coming! Needless to say we were glad to finally get off that train thirty-six hours later.

There's another train I'm glad I stepped off years ago. I call it the crazy train. That week I talked with a friend who was walking through a difficult time. As we talked I began to hear some similar issues and failed methods that I had walked through in my own life. Like me, my friend had hooked his life up to the crazy train. The crazy train is when we hook our personal value to the acceptance or rejection of other people and/or our success or failure. It goes something like this.

This emotional train goes up the hill when: someone praises you, accepts you, adds you on social media, recognizes your hard work, invites you, when the opposite sex desires you or needs you, or when you win or succeed.

The train goes downhill when: people stop praising you, don't friend you, stop inviting you, stop giving you recognition, don't call you, when the opposite sex doesn't desire you, when it seems no one needs you, when someone's upset with you, when you fail or lose.

You can understand why people hook up to this train. The highs are surreal and it feels great; as if you could do no wrong. However, the downside to the crazy train is a steep one. If you're hooked up to this train, the valley is horrifically painful when your pipeline of acceptance and love from people or success is cut off.

So what's the remedy? You can't get off the track of life. Your life is going to be hooked to someone or something regardless. The lifesaving alternative is to hook your life up to

Jesus Christ. Your definition in Him isn't based on your performance or people's high or low view of you. You don't have to go any farther than Jesus Christ to find an ocean of love and acceptance waiting for you. Take it from a guy that was hooked to the crazy train for a long time: spinning out when people didn't like me or disagreed with me, rocketing skyward on well-intentioned compliments, free falling toward depression when it seemed I failed. Pull the pin on this dysfunctional locomotive that's pulling you up and down and hook your life up to Jesus who is faithful, steady and reliable.

You don't have to go any farther than Jesus Christ to find an ocean of love and acceptance waiting for you.

The Apostle Paul makes the case that we must put all of our thoughts under the truth and authority of Christ:

2 Corinthians 10:5:

We destroy arguments and every lofty opinion raised against the knowledge of God, and take every thought captive to obey Christ . . .

When you find yourself stuck in fear and discouragement take those thoughts captive. How? Ask yourself, "What's my biggest fear right now?" "What do I feel powerless to change?"

The idea here is to discover the core thought that is driving your fear, worry, and discouragement. Once you have that answered ask yourself, "What does God have to say about that? What does he say He will do for me? What are his promises? How does He tell me to respond in this moment? What does faith say?

Let me give you an arsenal of scripture to respond with when fear and discouragement come knocking. Feel free to put them on Post-it notes in your bathroom, office, or car. Whatever you do, keep them in front of you during such a season.

2 Timothy 1:7:

. . . for God gave us a spirit not of fear but of power and love and self-control.

Philippians 4:6–7:

. . . do not be anxious about anything, but in everything by prayer and supplication with thanksgiving let your requests be made known to God. And the peace of God, which surpasses all understanding, will guard your hearts and your minds in Christ Jesus.

Hebrews 13:6:

So we can confidently say, "The Lord is my helper; I will not fear; what can man do to me?"

God's word is most effective in our lives when applied. It's not enough to do an emotional and spiritual assessment and understand what's going on, we must apply God's truths to our thinking and faith. Imagine a doctor that only diagnoses, but doesn't treat the disease. That's ridiculous.

With these scriptures you now have a response for that fear and discouragement as you send them packing out the door.

We need to look to God's word daily as our life-compass that gives us a true north. If you were on a journey where you were traveling every day, you wouldn't only look at your compass once a week! No, you'd be looking every day, many times a day; to make sure you're headed in the right direction.

A passage in the book of Lamentations reminds me of this thought. After the prophet Jeremiah lists all his grievances, of how terrible life seems to be going, and how horrible his circumstances, he says this . . .

Lamentations 3:21–23:

But this I call to mind, and therefore I have hope: The steadfast love of the LORD never ceases; his mercies never come to an end; they are new every morning; great is your faithfulness.

Jeremiah's response to his discouraging circumstances was to "call to mind" God's character of faithfulness. You must have the truth *in you* to be able to "call it to mind" in the midst of your discouragement. We need God's power and grace to apply his word to our thought life.

We also need people in our lives that can point us to God's truth when we get sideways, discouraged and withdrawn. Who is in your life that will say, "Hey! You're not alone! That's not true! God is faithful! Let's turn to Him! Let's see what He will do!"

Do you want to see your faith level rise? Begin to hang out with some eagles of faith. Stop allowing your deepest relationships to be with lame turkeys in the faith. Who you fly with matters!

When you're discouraged you must draw a line in the sand and refuse to bow down to self-pity. No one wants to be a quitter, but we've all felt the temptation to want to throw in the towel. I heard this fitting quote years ago, "When you throw a pity party, the devil always shows up with balloons and cupcakes!" Satan loves to pour gasoline on the fires of self-pity in our lives. He wants us to get so inward focused on our own inadequacies that we stop looking to God's sufficiency.

I was on one of my runs this last winter, and I was in the last quarter-mile when I faced a grueling hill on the way home. My legs were on fire and my lungs felt like they were breathing fire as I lumbered through the thirty-two degree weather. As I looked toward the top of the hill a little voice chimed in, "You've run well, you don't have to do this. This hill is too steep after the run you've had. Just walk it in." The quitter inside me wanted to call it a day. In fact, he always wants to have a say when life gets tough. I know his voice well.

What about you? I don't know what your steep hill looks like these days, but you do. Where are you feeling like playing the quitter card? Maybe it's your marriage, your job, your ministry, school, a relationship, your health . . . maybe just life in general.

Don't you dare! God has something God glorifying for you on the other side of that hill. The Apostle Paul writes one of the most powerful sentences in the Bible for how to approach life. Here it is:

Be joyful in hope, patient in affliction, faithful in prayer (Rom. 12:12).

This one sentence holds three keys to persevering through discouragement:

1. **Keep Hope Alive:** The moment we give up our hope for better God-given outcomes, despair sweeps in. "I can't" and "there's no way" become our mantra. Remember your hope isn't in yourself anyway, it's in Christ.

2. **Be patient in the pain:** As I was running up that hill I realized that I was going to have to endure the pain in my legs and lungs for only a little while if I wanted to make it to the top. As I ran, I remembered other times when I had pushed past the pain and conquered. If I was patient in the pain, I could kick the hill in the teeth. I had to remember my hill wouldn't last forever; neither will yours.

3. **Stay Faithful in Prayer:** I know what you're thinking, "Thanks for the real unique advice to pray." But let me push back on you for a moment. Long before we quit life's challenges, we quit praying. In doing so, we stop listening to God about what He thinks about our situation and start listening to ourselves, others, and our culture. Prayer is the most under-utilized weapon we have in our arsenal as followers of Christ. Countless times in my life, when life has hit the fan, I've made an all too familiar mistake: I've counted on myself to get me through it. I've chosen to lean on my intellect, strength, and talent. But, here's the problem. There's not much there. They always fall short. And it's

not just me that pays the price. My family, friends, and ministry take a hit too. In fact, most of my life problems have come from me looking other places besides the Lord for help.

Can you relate?

You very well might believe that Christ's death and resurrection is enough to save you for eternity, but do you trust Him with your present day life: your family, your finances, your health, your calling, your future? Or do you merely see Christ as the one getting heaven ready and until then you're on your own? God offers you more than an eternity with Him, he offers you a refuge in Him: right here . . . right now.

Let me share with you these words written by King David:

This God—his way is perfect; the word of the Lord proves true; he is a shield for all those who take refuge in him. For who is God, but the Lord? And who is a rock, except our God?— the God who equipped me with strength and made my way blameless (Psalm 18:30–32).

"He is a shield for all those who take refuge in him . . ." Get this! The God of the universe offers Himself as your shield, your comforter, and sustainer. Why would you go anywhere else? Our tendency to clamor for other "tangible" remedies leaves us bankrupt of the comfort God offers through prayer. If we're going to endure this test, we must no longer see prayer as a chore, but as a lifeline to the Father when we need Him most. God wants to speak life into you! Talk to Him.

Prayer is the most under-utilized weapon we have in our arsenal as followers of Christ.

Next time the quitter inside you speaks up, shove an eviction notice in his loud mouth. God has you in the palm of His hand and is working ALL things out for your good. Keep your hope alive in Him. Stay patient in the pain and keep sharing your heart with Him in prayer.

Keep. Going.

KEYS TO REMEMBER

Ever feel like you are one step from triumph and one step from the wheels coming off the tracks at the same time? For those of us that find ourselves emotionally wrapped up in what we "do" it can seem like there's a thin line between feeling like a victor or a victim. When I begin to feel like I'm teetering on that line I make an effort to remember three things:

1. **Life is seasonal:** As a pastor I have to constantly remind myself that my life is full of seasons: in our church, my family, myself, in the lives of others. As much as we'd like to we can't park at one perfect spot in life. The writer of Ecclesiastes nails this idea when he writes: "For everything there is a season, and a time for every matter under heaven" (Eccl. 3:1). Deep down we know this, but it can be easy

to forget when we're in the midst of a down time.
It feels like we've been here forever and things will
never change. That's just not true. Do this: reflect
on the various down seasons in your life that you've
walked through. What were the nuggets of truth
that you picked up during that time? Choose to see
the wins and the wisdom God has given you.

2. **Obstacles Can Bring New Possibilities:** Author
   Michael Hyatt writes, "One of the best questions
   you can ask when something negative happens is
   this: What does this make possible?" Asking this
   question allows you to take another look at your
   circumstances in a positive light. Seriously, try
   it. If you're honest there most likely is an upside
   to the situation: more time with the family, less
   pressure at work, an opportunity to learn a new
   profession or trade, it could be anything! What
   you see as a negative, God is working for your
   good (Romans 8:28).

3. **You are not the sum of your successes or failures:**
   We tend to fall into the trap of one side or the other.
   We either define ourselves by what we've achieved
   or by how we've blown it. This is a double-edged
   sword. While we may feel great when things are
   riding high, we feel like we need to be on suicide
   watch when things hit the tank. We have to be
   careful not to hook ourselves up to the crazy train of
   our emotions. Your value can't be measured by your
   success in money, number of clients, promotions,
   Facebook likes, attendance, acclaim . . . the list goes

on. If you hook your self-worth to external inputs you're headed for a train wreck. Your value doesn't come from what you've made of yourself, but from who made you, God himself.

Here are some forward leaning actions to take when discouragement has hijacked your life:

Share: Don't default to isolation and throwing yourself a pity party. Over the years I've watched countless people withdraw into themselves and move away from the people that care about them most. Satan will try to tempt you to believe that "no one will understand" and "you're the only one going through this" or "no one cares" . . . they're all lies. Take some time to share with a trusted fellow Christian how you're feeling and allow them to give you some encouragement and perspective.

Go: We can sometimes default to performing an unending autopsy of our circumstances. Like trying to peel layers of a never ending onion, we find the job is never finished. If you've taken time to reflect and learn from your circumstances it's time to move forward. Get moving!

Cast: The apostle Peter gives us a pivotal action step that we'll need to employ every time we encounter these ongoing burdens of life:

1 Peter 5:6–7:

Humble yourselves, therefore, under the mighty hand of God so that at the proper time he may exalt you, casting all your anxieties on him, because he cares for you.

If you're going to be able to truly move forward, you're going to have to lighten the load of life. Peter gives us a directive to "cast your anxieties" on Jesus. The reason we're called to throw off these anxieties is because we're not designed to carry them. We were originally designed to be completely dependent on God for every part of our lives. Since sin entered the picture mankind has sought to control outcomes and survive without God. The result has been mankind turning themselves into their own pack mules for their burdens. You weren't meant to be a beast of burden.

Peter writes, "Cast your anxieties on Him because He cares for you." Jesus not only longs to cover your sins, He longs to carry your burdens. If we can trust Christ with our eternal salvation, we can trust him with the here and now!

Recently I was jarred awake by my youngest son who ran into my room after waking up from a nightmare. After I talked with him about his dream, I prayed with him. As he wrapped his arms around me he said, "Dad, can I sleep in here?" "Sure", I said. After running to get his pillow, he climbed under the covers and I turned out the light. As we lay there for a moment he said, "Dad ... your hand." I reached out toward him and he took hold of it like a desperate drowning man clinging to a life-line just thrown to him.

Jesus not only longs to cover your sins, He longs to carry your burdens.

As he drifted off to sleep I was reminded by the comfort I've found in my heavenly father when walking through what seemed like a bad dream in life. God's words in the Bible have been a life preserver keeping me afloat when I've felt adrift on the open churning sea of my circumstances. Here is a verse I cling to:

Psalm 33:4

For the word of the Lord is upright, and all his work is done in faithfulness.

Though you may not see a ship in sight, know that the Captain of the ship has not forgotten you. Cling to His Word. He will not fail you. He . . . is . . . faithful.

CHAPTER 8

MY EXPERTISE: FAILURE

Failures, repeated failures, are finger posts on the road
to achievement. One fails forward toward success.

– C.S. Lewis

There aren't many subjects where I feel like an expert, but with this chapter on failure I feel right at home. On a regular basis I feel like the biggest hypocrite that's ever walked the planet. As a Christian husband, father, and pastor I'm constantly seeking to lead others toward full maturity in Christ, all the while seeing clearly my blatant moments of immaturity.

The list is long of instances when I've been an idiot and made poor choices. From the mundane to the profound, I've made some doozies. Picture this, I'm driving down the road on the way to the office and I see a Texas Longhorn sticker on the back window of a guy's truck. Being out of Texas, I don't see a ton of these so I decided to let him know "I'm a Longhorn fan too!" I drive up next to him and proceed to give him the "hook'em horns" sign with my hand, but surprisingly the guy looks at me like I'm nuts. I'm thinking, what's the deal, show me some love! What I then realize is that instead of the "hook'em horns" sign (raised forefinger and pinky), I was giving him the "I LOVE YOU" sign (thumb, forefinger, pinky). As he quickly accelerated, I felt again that my actions once again confirmed that I'm an idiot.

Here's the deal, as I said before that story pales in comparison to some of the other things I've done in my life. When I look back at the moments that I've fallen on my face and blown it, there is always a wave of guilt and shame that rushes over me. It can be crippling and made me feel like I could never move forward.

Of all people, my wife has the privilege of holding a lifetime season pass with a front row seat to my daily blowouts as a Christian: my selfishness, my overreacting, my underreacting, my tunnel vision, my lack of vision, etc. The list goes on. (See Erin for more details)

There's an ongoing feeling of inadequacy of being able to be the man my wife and boys deserve. Ever feel that way? Crouching at my door every day is this nagging temptation: "Stop caring, stop leading . . . give up. If you can't lead yourself, then stop trying to lead others."

Thankfully we find one of the great pillars of the Christian Church, the Apostle Paul, speaking to this very struggle inside each of us:

Romans 7:18-25:

For I have the desire to do what is good, but I cannot carry it out. For I do not do the good I want to do, but the evil I do not want to do—this I keep on doing. Now if I do what I do not want to do, it is no longer I who do it, but it is sin living in me that does it. So I find this law at work: Although I want to do good, evil is right there with me. For in my inner being I delight in God's law; but I see another law at work in me, waging war against the law of my mind and making me a prisoner of the law of sin at work within me. What a wretched man I am! Who will rescue me from this body that is subject to death? Thanks be to God, who delivers me through Jesus Christ our Lord!

If God can use the Apostle Paul (a self-confessed failure) to pen line upon line of eternal truth in scripture as well as take the Christian faith to the lost globally, he can use broken people like you and me. God chooses to use imperfect people like you and me to lead and love those around us. Read that sentence again.

God may not make junk, but he uses it every single day to show what He's able to work with. Why does He do this? Because in doing so He gets the glory for it all.

To me this is unbelievable, crazy, and humbling. So before you look for ways to meet the needs of your family, you need to first come to the understanding that He can do this through you. Let me encourage you not to get stuck worrying if your friends and family will ever be able to see you in that light. As we walk through this chapter, trust in God's word. Take some time in prayer to thank God for what He's going to do in your life, for what he has already done. Ask Him to allow you to be the conduit of love, strength and blessing to your family and friends as he's designed. I'm praying with you.

FAILURE: THE NEW NORMAL

Failure isn't something we like to talk about. In fact our current culture has a fixation on avoiding calling anyone or anything a failure. Take for instance the trophies they give out to Little League Baseball teams. When I was a kid if you didn't come in first, second, or third place you didn't get any type of trophy. Today, every kid gets a trophy just for participating. "Come in last place? No problem. Here's your trophy!" It's like telling a child, "You didn't strike out; you just hit the air really well!"

The reality: failure is normal. The Bible is riddled with men and women who blew it: Peter, Judas, David, Samson, Moses, Josiah, Solomon . . . all had moments of failure.

It's crucial that we look at our response to failure because it is something all of us have and will experience. As a pastor I've watched countless people become internally paralyzed by their mistakes and failures and end up on the side of the road stuck; merely going through the motions.

God wants you to be able to move through your failures with unstoppable faith as you tap in to his grace and wisdom.

Let me caution you to turn away from the temptation to buy into a "motivational speaker" way of thinking that somehow "we have inside of us all we need" and we just need to get up and try again. While that sounds great, it's not biblical. God wants our reliance on Him so that when we fail we are not just left with the broken pieces of ourselves falling short again in the end. How does God want us to view our failure as a husband, wife, mom, dad, business owner, friend, son, daughter, teacher, pastor?

As usual the Word of God has an answer for us. In the book of Philippians, Paul is writing to the local church in Phillipi about how he has come to view his past achievements as falling incredibly short of everything that He knows God has for Him. Paul has a Holy Discontent to know Christ and not rest on his past accomplishments, religious heritage, or what he has or hasn't done. He writes:

Philippians 3:12–14

Not that I have already obtained this or am already perfect, but I press on to make it my own, because Christ Jesus has made me his own. Brothers, I do not consider that I have made it my own. But one thing I do: forgetting what lies behind and straining forward to what lies ahead, I press on toward the goal for the prize of the upward call of God in Christ Jesus.

Paul states in humility twice, "I haven't arrived. I'm on this journey too." Paul speaks about this Holy Ambition of chasing down the man God has called Him to be. It's as if he's saying, "Because Jesus has made me His own, I'm pressing toward being made more like Him."

"This one thing I do" is actually a two step process:

1. "Forgetting what lies behind": This is his regrets.

Philippians 3:13

But one thing I do: forgetting what lies behind and straining forward to what lies ahead . . .

I love what Paul writes here, because you know he truly owns this. How many Christians had he watched die because of his actions? How many were torn from their families and suffered because of his actions? How many times did he say to himself, "Why did I do that? I wish I could go back."

I can relate with Paul. We all can. How many times have you said, "If I only would have . . . I wish I wouldn't have . . . My life would have been so much better if I hadn't . . ." These could be things we have done or not done. Unfortunately, no one has invented a time machine where mistakes can be undone.

People say, we're not defined by our failure. But we absolutely are! Read Paul's inspired words here:

Romans 3:23

for all have sinned and fall short of the glory of God

Our failures define us as those in desperate need of God's grace. We must get this; otherwise we begin to believe we're not in need of God's forgiveness and mercy. The truth is "no one is righteous, no not one" (Rom. 3:10). That means if you're reading this, you've already failed; you've fallen short of what God intended. That statement isn't written to discourage you, but simply remind you that we're all failures. You are not alone in your failure or your need for a forward looking remedy.

This isn't anything new. Adam and Eve were not only the first man and woman, they were also the first people to sin against God. Their initial sin has had a ripple effect the width of human history. As even now, each of us has been born into sin. Without this sin being dealt with, a fixed spiritual canyon separates us from God.

However, I've got great news. God, the Father, sent his only son, Jesus Christ to live a sinless life that you and I have been unable to live. He then died the death that you and I deserved; taking upon himself the just wrath of God for our sin. Incredibly he rose from the dead, conquering death, hell, and the grave so that now anyone that places their faith in Him (Christ) would be forgiven for their failures, given eternal life, and promised abundant life in the here and now.

Have you done that? Have you placed your faith in Christ? I'm praying that you will if you haven't already.

It is with this in mind that Paul goes on to write that there's a better destination to press on toward than staying here with our regrets:

> But one thing I do: forgetting what lies behind and straining forward to what lies ahead, I press on toward the goal for the prize of the upward call of God in Christ Jesus (Philippians 3:13–14).

I remember years ago hearing a famous story about Billy Graham, one of the greatest evangelists our country has produced. The story goes, one day during Graham's early years of traveling and speaking, he was passing through a small town when he was pulled over for speeding. In those days it wasn't uncommon if you were from out of town to have to stand before the judge the very day you were pulled over. Billy had to do just that.

As he stood before the judge and the speeding citation was read before the court, the judge asked Graham if he had indeed been speeding that morning. He responded, "I am guilty your Honor." Just then the judge recognized Graham's voice and face. The judge replied, "Because of your guilt, the fine must be paid. However, I'm happy to pay it for you." The judge reached into his black robe and pulled out his wallet where he proceeded to pay the court clerk the fine. Not only that, he insisted on treating Billy to a steak dinner! It was at this steak dinner that Billy exclaimed, "This is a perfect picture of God's grace. I was absolutely guilty and someone stepped in and freely paid what was due!"

If you've leaned your entire life on Jesus, placing your faith in him, your sin has been forgiven. It's here that I'm reminded of the countless times I've heard people say to me, "I hear that you're saying God's forgiven me, but I can't seem to forgive myself." Let me be clear here: to not forgive yourself isn't noble, it's idolatry. You are trying to put yourself in God's role as judge and decide when you are and are not forgiven. God doesn't need your help. He's been doing this a long time. Who are you to decide when someone is or is not forgiven? When we refuse to receive God's forgiveness we're saying, "Jesus, your death and resurrection wasn't enough for me. I'm the exception to how far your grace can go." Receive Christ's forgiveness!

If you've placed your faith in Jesus not only has your sin been forgiven, it's been forgotten!

For as high as the heavens are above the earth, so great is his steadfast love toward those who fear him; as far as the east is from the west, so far does he remove our transgressions from us (Psalm 103:11–12).

Imagine that a friend of yours had a pet that died and they told of the elaborate burial that took place in their back-yard. While you didn't know the pet well, you knew it was upsetting to your friend. Then a few months go by without thinking any more about it until one day you go by this same friend's home to borrow a needed item. You knock on the front door and get nothing. Hearing your friend's voice in the back-yard you walk to the side of the house to see the gate ajar. As you move closer to the gate you see something shocking. Your friend has apparently dug up their once buried pet and is now trying to play with it as they did before.

Morbid . . . I know. Hang with me.

Christ has buried our sin, yet we love to continually res-urrect it. We have it in our heads that if we move on from our failure that means we've not taken it seriously. Yet, Jesus hasn't provided a way of freedom for us only to sit around and talk about the chains we should be wearing. That's why the Apostle Paul also wrote these words:

There is therefore now no condemnation for those who are in Christ Jesus. For the law of the Spirit of life has set you free in Christ Jesus from the law of sin and death (Romans 8:1–2).

I can hear some of you thinking at this point, "Nathan, is it truly possible to forget like Paul says?" Probably not. What Paul is saying here, "I'm choosing to change my focus; I'm moving my focus off my past and I'm focusing on Jesus. We must fix our eyes on Jesus, not our failure. When you feel tempted to go and dig up your past, remind yourself of God's grace by going to his word and prayer. Invite other mature believers into your failure. Allow them to remind you of God's love and mercy. This is one of the reasons God has provided the Church body.

God is glorified when we as failures come to Him and He walks us out of our pain. God gets the glory when a broken life is restored and forward growth takes place. God ultimately gets the glory because Jesus is the one who makes all things new.

My prayer is that you're beginning to see an incredible picture of God's grace as He deals with our failure. A patient God, slow to anger, exceeding in mercy. That's how God has chosen to lovingly deal with us.

LIFE BEYOND YOUR FAILURE

Many people believe the only thing that Jesus offers is forgiveness. That's not true. It certainly is part of what he offers, but he offers so much more. Paul shares with us that he's pressing toward the prize which is Christ, not just forgiveness from Him. Christ is the prize and with Him he offers forgiveness AND abundant life to all those that receive him.

The life bonus in all of this is that our failures don't have to be wasted. Like a phoenix rising from the ashes, our lives too can be better than they ever have been after failing. As a history buff my mind turns to a moment in America's Civil

War. After the brutal human toll and Confederate retreat at Gettysburg, General Robert E. Lee wrote a letter to Jefferson Davis, president of the Confederacy. He wrote: "We must expect reverses, even defeats. They are sent to teach us wisdom and prudence, to call forth greater energies, and to prevent our falling into greater disasters."

This is hard to fathom when read that historians put the Confederate casualties and losses at Gettysburg over twenty-three thousand. Yet, Lee wasn't downplaying the defeat, he was merely speaking to the benefits that defeats bring. The same is true for us. Our failures can be the very catalyst that keeps us from "falling into greater disasters."

Which brings me to this crucial point: Mature Christians allow failure to refine them, not just define them. The greatest tragedy of failure is not the failed act itself, but in not learning from our failures, not growing in wisdom, or Godly perspective.

When pride comes, then comes disgrace, but with the humble is wisdom (Proverbs 11:2).

We see countless times in the book of Proverbs a call for those that love God to seek wisdom. You and I compound our failures when we don't seek to grow and learn as we walk out of failures. The Apostle Paul calls us to this "forgetting of what lies behind", but this in no way keeps us from learning all we can from our past. The blessing is that Christ allows all of this to happen while being wrapped in his love and mercy with the knowledge that He has our future in his hands.

You can't go back and change your past, but you can go forward and allow God to change your future. Failure in this life isn't optional, but taking hold of God's grace is. You can be like most people that refuse to accept God's forgiveness and would rather collect the failures of their lives like trophies. These people love to revisit them often and in doing so slip into self-pity and self-hatred. I've personally learned that if Satan cannot tempt you into present sin, He'll try to get you fixated on your past sin.

This would be a good time for an uncomfortable connected thought. Maybe some of you collect the failures of others. Maybe you've collected them from your spouse, parents, children, friends, co-workers . . . you hold onto them so that you can verbally remind them of their failures. Can I encourage you to forgive and release them as you would want to be forgiven and released? Forgive them as the Lord has forgiven you.

Now, back to gleaning from your past.

I just walked out of an adoption dedication ceremony for a thirteen year old girl in our church. For her it was a long time coming, and a huge milestone for the family. Along with friends and family in the room, there were several hopeful kids in foster care that were waiting to be adopted themselves.

I was overwhelmed with heartache for these kids that didn't have a Mom or Dad to care for them or call them their own. As I prayed for the young lady that was being adopted, I reminded her that she does not have to live in the past. She doesn't have to be solely defined by where she's come from: abandoned and unwanted by her biological mother.

There are many that live their lives that way, living out

how they see themselves: broken, used up, spoiled goods that no one wants. They walk in their shame and guilt refusing to let go of their past and move forward. They've become so defined by their past that to let it go would mean giving up who they believe they are.

When we focus on the past (what we've done or what's been done to us) we essentially let our past hijack our future. This is like mentally and emotionally getting into a time machine every day trying to live in the past. Fixating on the past paralyzes our present. More than that it breaks down the relationships around us, robs us of our present purpose, thus killing our future.

Maybe the family you came from was a dysfunctional mess. Maybe choices you've made in the past still haunt your heart and mind. Can I tell you that your past is not bigger than God's love for you? God loves you in spite of where you've been and what you've done or even what's been done to you! He sent His son Jesus to suffer a gruesome death on the cross to take on your sin and shame.

There is a rightful place for godly sorrow. We should certainly own our mistakes, take them seriously, and yes, make restitution with others if needed. But do all of this with a heart leaning forward into the new future God has for you. The cross of Christ reminds us that our failures were inevitable and that only He can bring forgiveness and healing to our broken lives. With the cross in full view, ask yourself: will I get up and move forward or will I choose to stay here?

Put your faith in Jesus, turn from your past and embrace your brand new future with Christ! Know that God's best for your life includes redefining who you are with His love, mercy and forgiveness. Remember this: where you are going with Jesus is more important than where you've been on your own. Stop living in the past and get back to the present.

CHAPTER 9

THE POWER OF YOUR STORY

Find out how much God has given you and from it take what you need; the remainder is needed by others.

—Saint Augustine

E veryone grows up wanting to be a hero. We want to make an impact on the world. I know I did. Growing up I heard stories of my grandfather serving as a soldier in the Second World War. Being around him as much as I was, I found myself wanting to serve in the Army as he did when my later high school years came around. This, combined with my youth driven search for adventure, made me putty in the hands of Army recruiters. When I signed on the dotted line to become a Combat Medic in my junior year of high school, the recruiter must have wished every kid went in that easily.

The United States Army plays on that ambition in young adults. If you take a look at old Army recruitment posters and commercials throughout the decades, you'll see a common thread in all of them: adventure, life purpose, and courage.

As we wrap up this book, I want to go into recruiting mode. I want to call you to something bigger than yourself and in doing so be someone's hero. You cultivating an unstoppable faith in the midst of your circumstances is a life long journey. It will never be completed. But what if along the way you could help others do the same? Wouldn't that redeem all the storms you've been through?

Part of the soldier's creed a soldier is asked to adopt is this: "I will never leave a fallen comrade." My platoon had this creed put to the test in a live fire exercise one night when we were training at Fort Lawton, Oklahoma. The field exercise consisted of navigating obstacles and ambushes in the shortest amount of time. There were parallel courses, and our platoon was pitted against a rival platoon that we'd been neck and neck with throughout our time there. Our platoon was highly competitive and we were hungry for a win.

A siren went off giving us the signal to start. We shot out as one knocking out the initial obstacles without any problem. Someone could see out of the corner of their eye that we were ahead of the other platoon. We then made our way to a barbed-wire crawl that was about fifty yards in length with live machinegun fire above our heads. (It's impossible your adrenaline not to be pumping when you're in this environment.) Most of us had big smiles on our faces as we couldn't believe we were actually being paid for this!

All of that smiling came to a halt as one of our fellow privates yelled out, "Where's Johnson!?" Each of us looked around; calling out to him. No response. We knew what we had to do. We knew that if we went on ahead we could win the competition, but if we left our comrade behind we'd lose more than the competition, we'd lose our honor. That wasn't an option. We had to go back for him.

We did.

We lost the training competition, but we won the hearts and minds of one another. Each of us knew that we had each other's back. And in war that goes a long way.

I'm asking you to take on this same "leave no one" behind creed with those around you. What I'm asking isn't easy. In fact, it can be downright terrifying, but I believe God longs to give us the courage to go back for the wounded people in our lives.

With this in mind, let me fill your courage tank for a moment.

Courage (kərij): mental or moral strength to venture, persevere, and withstand danger, fear, or difficulty

There's a difference between being courageous when faced with physical danger and having courageous character. One demands courage for a moment, the other a lifetime. In the face of physical dangers in various parts of the world, public ridicule, and going against cultural norms; we can see that courage in the life of a Christian is needed more than ever. Then there's battling that internal voice that we've all heard that says, "There's no way, it's not realistic, You could never do that, How could we afford that?"

Check out this snapshot of biblical courage of another soldier named Joshua as he takes over the leadership of Israel after Moses has died.

Joshua 1:5–7:

No man shall be able to stand before you all the days of your life. Just as I was with Moses, so I will be with you. I will not leave you or forsake you. Be strong and courageous, for you shall cause this people to inherit the land that I swore to their fathers to give them. Only be strong and very courageous, being careful to do according to all the law that Moses my servant commanded you. Do not turn from it to the right hand or to the left, that you may have good success wherever you go.

Three times God tells Joshua, "Be Strong and Courageous." Apparently this is something Joshua needed to hear. But why? He had already led the people in to battle countless times as their military leader. The answer may be found in who Joshua was following: Moses. Listen to how Moses' leadership is summed after He died.

Deuteronomy 34:10–12:

And there has not arisen a prophet since in Israel like Moses, whom the Lord knew face to face, none like him for all the signs and the wonders that the Lord sent him to do in the land of Egypt, to Pharaoh and to all his servants and to all his land, and for all the mighty power and all the great deeds of terror that Moses did in the sight of all Israel.

How would you like to follow that act? When I came to Radiant Church in Raleigh, NC to take my first senior pastor position, all I heard for the first six months was what an amazing leader the founding pastor was. He seemed to be a legend of biblical and mythical proportions! When I first met him, I wanted to ask him if he could indeed walk on water!

The fact is there can be a ton of internal pressure that comes with trying to keep up with the success of others. It also doesn't help that we tend to think that God is only with those that have more spiritual charisma, talent, intelligence, or that he's only with spiritual leaders. Joshua was no different. He needed the encouragement that since God was with Moses, God was with Him.

Which brings us to this truth: Godly courage is not the result of a position or title, but of faith. If you've put your faith in Jesus Christ as the savior and leader of your life, God is with you. Stand up. Be Bold. Be Strong and Courageous!

You are going to need that courage if you're going to make sure the pain in this life doesn't go to waste. Years ago that would have been hard for me to write. There was a time when I believed absolutely nothing could make up for some of the pain I've endured.

My legs felt like jelly the first time I stepped on to a church platform to share my story of abuse openly with a congregation. It seemed that all the moisture in my mouth had made its way to my palms; so much so that I almost dropped my Bible. Several times as I moved through my message notes, I entertained the idea of skipping over my story. I told myself, "No one will even know you left this out. There's still time to escape!" Thankfully, in spite of these feelings of dread, I opened my mouth and began to share.

I told them that when I was eight years old, I was sexually

abused by a grade school teacher and then again later on by a janitor at a daycare center. I told them that for years I felt I had some sort of sign on me that said, "Hurt me. I'm your target." I pushed on and shared the overwhelming sense of shame I felt. I told them even though I had done nothing wrong I always felt like I had; that it was somehow my fault. I walked around in constant fear that someone would find out.

My stomach was in knots as I opened up about the truth that these painful episodes led to a broken view of myself, women, and God. For years, I could only leave broken people in my wake. I was hurting, selfish, and angry. There was no fidgeting, no coughing. Just silence.

I then got to share with them when the sun came up. God in his goodness and mercy shined a light on my numb, parched heart. Through Christ, I found that not only were my sins covered through the cross, but so was my shame. Slowly, in time, forgiveness came for those that hurt me. "Now God has asked of me the unthinkable: to comfort those with similar stories. I'd like to pray with those that might be here that have a similar story." I prayed for peace, hope and healing for those anonymously hurting in the room. I closed the service in prayer as usual and came off the platform relieved that it was over. I noticed that my fear still clung to me because I couldn't look anyone in the eye.

Every bit of that remaining fear melted away as I looked across the room. Countless people were lining the aisles from three directions. Most were in tears as they grabbed my hand or reached out for a hug to say statements of gratitude or relief, "Thank you for saying out loud what I've wanted to say out loud for years", "I've kept this secret for so long", "I honestly felt like I was the only one", "I had given up any hope for living a normal life. You've given me hope that God has a future for me . . . ." And they kept coming. I was dumbstruck.

For some the idea that the horrific sexual abuse I endured when I was a child could be of any future value to me or anyone else seems ludicrous and sick. Little did I know that God was going to build a bridge of hope for others with my testimony. And yet here I am, having shared my story countless times with people hurting under similar circumstances.

In all of this God has taught me a profound truth: The comfort God gives us in our suffering isn't just for us.

Read the words of the Apostle Paul:

2 Cor. 1:3–5:

Blessed be the God and Father of our Lord Jesus Christ, the Father of mercies and God of all comfort, who comforts us in all our affliction, so that we may be able to comfort those who are in any affliction, with the comfort with which we ourselves are comforted by God. For as we share abundantly in Christ's sufferings, so through Christ we share abundantly in comfort too.

Did you catch that? God "comforts us in all our affliction" so that "we may be able to comfort those who are in affliction, with the same comfort . . ." When shared with others, God's comforting hand in our painful story can be a much needed beacon of hope for someone walking in darkness.

Years ago I was at Fort Jackson, SC going through the Army's Chaplain Training Course. One night in the pouring rain I was on another live fire training course. I was crawling face down in sand, in the rain, with all my gear including a heavy armor plated vest; all of this while crawling two hundred yards. At first when we came climbing out of the trench I was pumped and excited and the adrenaline was flowing, but after about fifty yards my body caught up with my mind. Every part of my body was hurting (did I mention I had been up thirty-two hours at this point?) I continued to push on for about another 100 yards and had another fifty to go when everything within me said, "I'm done". My heart felt like it was going to explode . . . my muscles were cramped, and I rolled over on my back and cried out to God (literally) as these loud artillery shells were going off. As I did, Sergeant Ruiz at the end of the course began to call my name and told me to keep pushing. He yelled, "I've been right where you are! You can make it! Keep moving forward! Keep pushing through the pain!" His encouragement stirred me to dig deep and finish the course when I thought all of my resources were depleted.

We need more people like Sergeant Ruiz that have been through the war zone of life. That are willing to comfort those struggling by looking back and saying, "I've been where you are. You can make it!" You can share this comfort in countless ways. Share a scripture that held you up in the midst of your own pain. Share about the peace of God that came when peace seemed unattainable. Share about God's perfect timing and how he came through. Share how he's still walking you out of the woods. Don't make the mistake of thinking that God's comfort for you is only for you.

CONCLUSION

My family and I have been hidden away in the mountains of North Carolina for the last few days. It's been a much needed get away for all of us. I'm writing this last part in the cool of the morning on the back deck of the cabin we've been staying in.

Writing a book is hard. I'm not talking about the writing itself. Anyone can discipline themselves to make the time to sit down and get it done. I'm talking about the massive emotional risk that comes with putting your work out to be consumed and evaluated by others. Multiply that risk exponentially if you choose to be transparent in writing about your own inadequacies and failures. Even the previous chapter that shares about my childhood abuse leaves me feeling naked in front of the iceberg.

I want you to know that I get it. Getting real about your

failures with others can feel daunting. Our fears can range from feeling like our transparency will only be wasted to being afraid that others might use our honesty against us in the future. Everyone knows that the temptation to try and fashion a persona of perfection for others is real, but we also know deep down that a crafted façade helps no one. When you risk big and choose to open up about where your struggles and God's grace meet, people are helped. You give them two wonderful gifts: fellowship in the midst of failure and hope for the future. To me, that's worth it all.

ABOUT THE AUTHOR

Nathan Rouse is first and foremost a pastor. He also is a husband, father, and author. He is lead pastor at Radiant Church, a vibrant, growing church in Raleigh, NC. Though he currently lives in North Carolina, he still avidly roots for his favorite Texas sports teams.

Visit www.NathanRouse.org to discover
more of Nathan's work.

Nathan would also love to connect with you online:

Facebook: www.Facebook.com/NathanRousePage
Twitter: www.Twitter.com/NathanRouse
Instagram: www.Instagram.com/NathanRouse1

NOTES

Chapter 3

1. Lewis, C.S. Mere Christianity. New York City: Harper Collins, 2001.

Chapter 4

1. Osbeck, K.W. Amazing Grace: 366 Inspiring Hymn Stories for Daily Devotions. Grand Rapids: Kregal Publications, 1996.